FRANK LLOYD WRIGHT

INTERIOR STYLE & DESIGN

FRANK LLOYD WRIGHT

INTERIOR STYLE & DESIGN

DOREEN EHRLICH

COURAGE
BOOKS
AN IMPRINT OF
RUNNING PRESS BOOK PUBLISHERS

Philadelphia • London

Printed and bound by Imago in Singapore

9 8 7 6 5 4 3 2 1
Digit on the right indicates the number of this printing

Library of Congress Control Number
2002116603

ISBN 0-7624-1627-0

Produced by
PRC Publishing Ltd,
The Chrysalis Building,
Bramley Road, London W10 6SP

A member of **Chrysalis** Books plc

Published by Courage Books, an imprint of
Running Press Books Publishers
125 South Twenty-second Street
Philadelphia, Pennsylvania 19103-4399

Visit us on the web!
www.runningpress.com

Page 2: The library at the Frank Lloyd Wright Home and Studio.

CONTENTS

INTRODUCTION

Style and design were a defining part of

Frank Lloyd Wright's work and influence, from the earliest designs for houses in the 1890s, when he was in his twenties, to his final work in both the private and public domain in the late 1950s. His idea of an organic architecture required furnishings that would be an integral part of their spatial environment. He began his career with a radical reworking of the private space of the family, using his own home and studio practice in Oak Park, Illinois, as a laboratory in which to experiment with the changing needs of his growing family. He was to rearrange the furniture and objects in this and later houses at least twice a year and even to transfer the practice to client's houses in his continuous search for the qualities of harmony and repose he prized above all others.

Wright's building commissions and clients were many and various, yet for each one certain factors were crucial. Each was designed to be site specific, the location and surrounding setting were both vital, as were the economic circumstances and individual needs of the client or clients. Fixtures and furnishings, together with both interior ornament and detail were particular to each project. In his pursuit of the totally integrated organic environment, Wright regarded each design component together with the walls and ceilings, each chair and lighting fixture,

Above right: Frank Lloyd Wright Home and Studio, Oak Park Illinois. Name plaque at entrance to the studio. The bas relief was sculpted by Richard Bock to Wright's design and includes the distinctive emblem of a circle inscribed in a square.

Right: Frank Lloyd Wright at work c. 1915. Platinum print by Eugene Hutcheson.

Right: Frank Lloyd Wright Home and Studio, Oak Park, Illinois. North bedroom. Simplicity and a sense of repose were essential qualities of the Wright domestic interior. Here these qualities are typified in the uncluttered space, the undisguised use of natural materials and the flow of natural light in a high-ceilinged space.

6

as a matrix of the whole. Extraordinary attention was paid to the smallest details of the total environment, whether it be the detail of the light fittings in a domestic interior or a public space: the high-backed chairs for a family meal or the office chairs that were to determine the posture of the staff in the Johnson Wax Administration Building were equally worthy of his attention. The spindle-back chairs around his family dining table at Oak Park were the first in a long line of development and exist in a set of eight. Half a century later, the tubular Johnson chairs were serially produced but only for use in the building for which they were designed and are still in use today.

Wright's earliest work included public buildings such as Unity Temple, which entailed a radical rethinking of the form and function of a religious structure, and extends through designs for work environments, such as the Johnson Wax Administration Building and the Marin County Civic Center, to such iconic buildings as the Solomon Guggenheim Museum, New York, completed in 1959. Such total environments are Wright's major contribution to the history of architecture, although it should be remembered that several of his most remarkable achievements in the public domain no longer exist and can only be studied from photographs and from surviving fragments.

These key buildings include the Imperial Hotel Tokyo, the Larkin Office Building, and Midway Gardens, Chicago. The Midway Gardens entertainment complex of 1913, which was razed in 1929, is a particularly sad loss, as it provided Wright with the opportunity to design an elaborate decorative scheme of extraordinary innovation and variety in each and every detail, down to the last coffee cup. Fortunately other public buildings such as the Johnson Wax Administration Building are still in use and the great majority of his domestic buildings have been carefully preserved, with many being accessible to the public.

Although Wright has been considered a contradictory architect in many ways, he was consistent in his major concern of breaking down the "box" of room spaces in conventional buildings and of dissolving, where appropriate, the apparent distinction between the building and its surrounding area. The integration of each and every design element, together with the qualities of harmony and repose are the keynotes of Wright's style and design. His insistence on the organic nature of each building, and his own control of the design components of each space resulted in unusually integrated designs. This control extended to the design not only of the built-in and free-standing furniture but such elements as the windows, carpets, and even the kettle on the hearth, in the case of Fallingwater, and Wingspread, for example. The Prairie houses, which first brought him fame at home and abroad, included Wright-designed built-in furniture, lighting fixtures, textiles, and carpets that used the same motifs as the window glass. It was even said that Wright's concern for the detail demanded by organic architecture led him to design dresses for his female clients at Oak Park so that their dinner-party clothes should harmonize with the décor.

Photographs exist of Catherine Tobin Wright wearing dresses of a geometric cut that seem to correspond with John Lloyd Wright's description of his father's dress designs ("Papa designed most of Mama's dresses. Most of Mama's dresses were brown!"), thus harmonizing with the paneling and subdued lighting of the quintessential Wright interior of the period.

Left: The Imperial Hotel Tokyo, interior. Wright's work on the massive hotel occupied him from 1916 to 1922. The design for the total environment included such components as furniture, murals, and ceramics.

Left: Photograph of Catherine Tobin Wright in a dress designed for her by her husband, 1908. The geometric design of the bodice and sleeves has similarities to Wright's art-glass patterns.

9

Left: Kenneth Laurent House, Rockford, Illinois. The first of the solar hemicycle houses, designed around the idea of a "football plan." Wright's client was confined to a wheelchair and the house was adapted to his needs, including uninterrupted access to this gallery, which runs the length of the house.

From the beginning, Wright was always conscious of the needs of his clients and would incorporate these into his work where possible, although such collaborations were not always straightforward. Wright was to record some of these negotiations in *An Autobiography*, detailing for example, the progress of the Californian textile block house, the "Hollyhock House," while he was working in Japan on the Imperial Hotel, Tokyo. Wright described the "agonizing triangle" of owner, architect, and contractor, noting finally that "somehow by way of downright brutality, insolence, and persistence the architect and client's desire, though both architect and client were torn to tatters…form got into the building in spite of all folly."

In a changed world, 20 years later, each low cost Usonian home was adapted to the wishes of its owner who was asked to supply a "wants list" before the house was constructed, which Wright accommodated in the finished design.

The bespoke houses could accommodate needs as various as a living room that could be used as a space for performing chamber music, which Wright supplied with a specially designed music stand, or storage cupboards for home preserved produce that were accessible to an owner who was 5 feet 2 inches.

Wright was always open to interesting and unusual requests from prospective clients: one of the most striking and sympathetic responses to an individual's needs may be seen in Wright's design for the house for Kenneth Laurent in Rockford, Illinois, in 1949. Mr Laurent had written to Wright on seeing the first Usonian designs, explaining that he was a paraplegic and confined to a wheelchair but was attracted to the idea of an open-plan accessible house. Wright's response was to adapt the Usonian plan to a solar hemicycle, designed around the idea of a "football" plan, forming a longitudinal axis, with an elongated gallery extending almost the entire length of the house. He also included tiny but all important details in response to his client's special needs, so that, for instance, the inset lighting fixtures can be worked from a wheelchair using a tassel pull.

This close working relationship with his clients may be seen in Wright's very earliest commissions, the so-called "bootleg houses,"

Right: Frank Lloyd Wright Home and Studio, Oak Park, Illinois. Stork plaque at entrance to the studio. The four plaques were sculpted by Richard Bock from designs by Wright and show storks as symbols of fertility, flanking a plan of the Roman Baths of Caracalla.

Above: Frank Lloyd Wright Home and Studio, Oak Park, Illinois. The studio has a grand and complex entranceway for clients, presenting itself to the street as a series of vertical forms built of brick.

begun while he was working out his apprenticeship with the leading Chicago architectural firm of Adler and Sullivan. As his reputation grew, his client base changed to reflect the growing prosperity of the times. Wright was able to supply his clients with fully integrated living spaces, often with a single motif, such as the sumac plant, which provided the basis for the design of the art-glass, furniture, and other elements of the house built for Susan Lawrence Dana in 1902. The house, perhaps the finest and certainly the most elaborate of Wright's Prairie designs was intimately related to its site, a major characteristic of Wright's work throughout his life and one bound up with his idea of an organic architecture. Some Prairie houses, like the Dana House, were built on unprepossessing suburban sites, and here it was Wright's radical concept of the "vista within" that became all important. The richness of the house's glass ornamentation, both in the art-glass windows and in its specially designed and integrated light fixtures and fittings compensates for the lack of a natural vista on the site, which Wright called "the vista without," that forms such a spectacular part of many of his later buildings and brings nature inside.

In his commissions for offices and public buildings, where it was often crucial to create an inward looking space, as in the case of Unity Temple and the Johnson Wax Administration Building, Wright used concrete and glass to achieve a flow of natural light while ingeniously shielding the interiors from the noise and distractions of the world outside. The use of concrete in these and other buildings is an especially interesting example of Wright's innovative use of materials. Undisguised concrete had been regarded as a useful but low status material, albeit one that had been used since Roman times, where it had always been faced with costlier material.

Wright described concrete as "the cheapest (and ugliest) thing in the building world." He was attracted to the material by its plasticity, it would be, as he described it "susceptible to the impress of imagination." This can be seen structurally in the radical, light-filled designs of Unity Temple and the Johnson Wax Administration Building, and both structurally and decoratively in the textile block construction of the houses of the 1920s, he termed the California Romanza, such as the "Hollyhock House." The textile block construction, which was both

versatile and economical, could also be used to create its own spatial lexicon, taking its motif from the block itself. In the "Hollyhock" and other houses this lexicon is carried through from the patterned blocks of the façade and interiors to such details as the furniture and art glass of the building.

The use of natural materials, in what was considered an "honest state," was a crucial factor in Wright's design ethos. Oak was a favored wood, together with walnut for paneling and built-in and free-standing furniture, although as fashions changed, the dark-stained woods of the Oak Park years gave way to lighter colorations.

The finest materials were also used wherever possible in public buildings, even for the smallest details—the cords for the lighting fixtures of Unity Temple were covered with gold silk to harmonize with the prevailing tones of the interior. Such "vistas within" in public spaces were as fully integrated as in the domestic space, with a unified color scheme and linking motifs that run throughout the buildings and their

Above: Jean and Paul R. Hanna House ("Honeycomb House"), Stanford, California. The hexagonal unit or honeycomb, which gives the house its popular name, is used throughout the design, both in its ground plan and elevation, as well as its interior and exterior detail.

contents, as seen from the Johnson Wax Administration Building as well as the vast complexes of the Marin County Civic Center of Wright's last years.

Wright's radical ideas and innovative use of materials are a constant in his long career, but his very longevity poses particular problems with regard to the understanding of his work. It is important to consider the context of his times across such an extraordinarily long and productive working life. His early houses, for example, may be regarded as representative of a key American decade of experiment and invention, which (although it is considered to have taken its inspiration from the European Arts and Crafts movement, with its emphasis on the use of handcrafted natural materials) should of necessity be regarded as specifically American, embodying as the buildings do, ideas of self-reliance and relationship both to society as a whole and to a specific locale.

The so-called "simple house" of the latter years of the nineteenth century was concerned with the ideas of health, leisure and the ethical dimensions of the domestic domain. Wright wrote in *An Autobiography* that he was designing houses "for the growth of the soul", and this aspect of his work has much in common with that of his American contemporaries, the brothers Henry Mather Greene and Charles Sumner Greene, although the buildings use materials, glass in particular, for different ends.

Wright's awareness of the work of his contemporaries, in the United States and Europe, is a significant feature throughout his long career. He was also exceptionally adept at promoting his own work both at home and abroad from the beginning. For example, the progressive American periodical *House Beautiful*, which espoused the cause of "Simplicity, Economy, and Appropriateness in the Home" brought his work to a wide audience, as did publication of his designs in the popular *Ladies Home Journal*. In Europe, his work was brought to the notice of contemporary architects as early as 1910 with the publication of the *Wasmuth Portfolios*, which presented a complete folio of Wright's buildings to date and put his work firmly on the international map, where it remained for the rest of his career. Wright kept himself up to date with

current developments in both the United States and Europe, although the relationship of his work to that of his contemporaries is a complex one. There are many parallels in his early work with that of the Glasgow architect Charles Rennie Mackintosh, whose work Wright would have been able to study in the influential magazine *The Studio*. Yet Wright was always to set himself apart from his contemporaries in characteristically uncompromising terms, whether implicitly in the design of his buildings or in his manifold writings.

Wright was to constantly revise the theories and practices learned in the years of his apprenticeship with the leading Chicago architectural practice of Adler and Sullivan in the 1890s. Wright owed a great deal to the work of his "Lieber Meister" Louis Sullivan, to whom he was apprenticed from 1888–93, and who imbued a philosophy of architecture that remained with Wright throughout his life.

In the years of his apprenticeship, Sullivan and his partner, Dankmar Adler, were working on one of their most distinctive and radical buildings, the 13-story, metal-framed Chicago Stock Exchange. The centerpiece, the two-story Trading Room has been reconstructed in the Art Institute of Chicago, where it provides an invaluable resource for the understanding of Sullivan's best known dictum "form follows function" and its influence on the work of Sullivan's most famous follower. The vibrant, naturalistic color scheme of the room's design employs a system of painted stencils in no less than 57 different colors in 15 related and repeating organic patterns. The motifs of the overall design are repeated in the glass of the skylights, providing natural light in a fully integrated interior that creates the idea of a verdant inward-looking space in the midst of the bustling city—a device later developed by Wright in countless buildings.

By the 1950s, when Wright was in his eighties, he felt the need to redefine organic architecture and design in what he described as a lexicon of nine terms. These range from a redefinition of the rallying cry of Sullivan (and such later International Style architects as Mies van de Rohe, Walter Gropius, and Le Corbusier), "form follows function", to the crucial nature of "ornament" and the nature of its integration with "space." Ornament was a term particularly detested by Wright's

Left: Bathroom of Stanley and Mildred Rosenbaum House, Florence, Alabama. One of three bathrooms, the space is paneled in cypress throughout and lit from above by skylights.

Internationalist contemporaries, it finds no place in the radical designs of Le Corbusier or in the work of such Bauhaus architects as Mies van de Rohe (whom Wright regarded as his enemies). Mies famously declared that "less is more," and his work from the Seagram building in New York to the design of the famous chrome and leather Barcelona chair stands in sharp contradistinction to that of Wright.

Wright's definition of "ornament" was a near mystical one: he compared it to the expression of emotion (as in the making of poetry), which enhances the building and becomes an integrated part of the whole. This emphasis on the complete integration of a design, and Wright's antipathy towards those he termed "the Bauhaus Boys," continued throughout his life. The owners of the Goetsch-Winckler House of 1938 recalled removing a Bauhaus-designed chair when Wright was about to call and replacing it when he was gone as they feared the architect's scorn at the intrusion of such an artefact of International Modernism into one of his houses.

In 1953, at the age of 86, Wright published his last, most complex redefinition of what were for him the two most crucial elements of architecture: space and light. In *The Future of Architecture* space was defined as "the continual becoming, invisible fountain from which all rhythms flow to which they must pass. Beyond time or infinity. The new reality which organic architecture serves to employ in building. The breath of a work of art." As he entered his nineties he believed that modern architecture lacked the qualities that could be conveyed by the appropriate use of such factors as space, light, function, and ornament. In his own words, "This modern architecture is organic architecture deprived of a soul." It is this "soul," and the human qualities implied in the term, that sets Wright's buildings apart from those of his Modernist contemporaries and does something to explain their continuing power and resonance today.

Although Wright lived to the age of 92, and is regarded as one of the twentieth century's greatest architects, his fundamental ideas and beliefs were formed at the end of the 19th century. In *An Autobiography*, Wright wrote with characteristic directness "Early in Life, I had to choose between honest arrogance and hypocritical humility, I chose the

Right: Frank Lloyd Wright Home and Studio, Oak Park, Illinois. Reception area of the Studio complex. The spectacular art-glass skylights exert a strong directional pull to the drafting room beyond.

former and have seen no occasion to change." Such boundless self-confidence, together with Wright's lifelong desire to seek harmony with nature in his work, is essentially of the late nineteenth century. His architectural ethos should be seen in the context of such key thinkers as Ralph Waldo Emerson (1802–82) and Henry David Thoreau (1817–62), whose works helped him to develop a view of architecture that took nature and organic forms for its models on which he was to draw throughout his long life.

Wright's young adulthood in Wisconsin was marked by the fact that his father, William Cary Wright, who was a preacher and musician, vanished without trace when he was 18, his only legacy to his son was his love of music, particularly Bach and Beethoven, and its performance. His father's abandonment was to sadly foreshadow Wright's desertion

of his wife, Catherine, and their six children some 24 years later. The decisive childhood influence on Wright was, however, that of his mother, Anna Lloyd-Jones Wright. Anna, who was of direct Welsh descent, took the motto of her family, "Truth against the world" and emphasized its importance to her only son. She was convinced from his earliest years that he was destined to become a great architect and sought every means in her power to make this possible.

Anna and her family were essentially of their time in their dedication to education and self-improvement. One of Wright's earliest built designs was for the first Hillside School of 1887, a progressive educational establishment run by two of his maternal aunts, near Spring Green, Wisconsin. The charming Romeo and Juliet windmill, which served the purpose of bringing water to the school, still stands.

Above: Frank Lloyd Wright Home and Studio, Oak Park, Illinois. Detail of art-glass skylight. The rectilinear motifs, and the gold, sage green, and russett tonalities are characteristic of the spectacular skylights of the Studio complex.

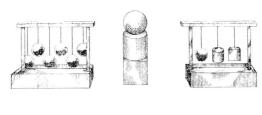

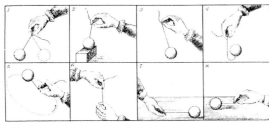

SECOND GIFT.

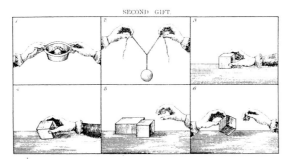

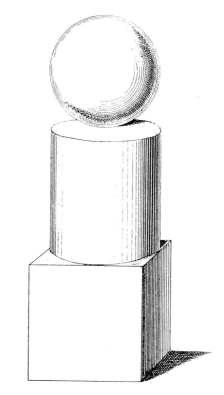

Right and above: The Froebel Gifts illustrated in *The Kintergarten Guide*, published in New York in 1886. The Gifts were presented to Wright as a child by his mother and were a crucial influence on his style and design throughout his life. The Cube, Cylinder, Sphere box, shown here, was particularly influential on his designs for furniture.

When Wright was a small child Anna and her sisters were much impressed by the Froebel system of kindergarten teaching, but lacked the means to attain it. However, even for mothers in straitened circumstances it was possible to provide the teaching tools of the system. These used the basic forms of nature, irreducible geometric shapes in both two and three dimensions, the so-called "Gifts." Wright's childhood experience of the "Gifts" had a profound influence on his work as he later acknowledged "…the modular system that has been the back of every design I ever made."

Froebel's system is dependent on learning by doing and the child learns the fundamental laws of nature by working with simple wooden blocks, and brightly colored cardboard shapes. Organic forms drawn from nature are reduced to abstract shapes. The influence of these abstracted cone, sphere, and cylinder forms can be seen in many of Wright's buildings, from the steep roofs and jutting eaves of the houses for some of his earliest clients to the Usonian houses of his last years, and indeed the fixtures and fittings of public and private buildings throughout his career.

The earliest style and design elements formed by the Froebel blocks are particularly aptly seen in the striking, barrel-vaulted playroom with its integrated toy cabinets and child-scaled furniture, designed for his own six children at Oak Park in 1895. Affectionate memories of the space and its contents remained with the children throughout their lives, as did the fact that they, along with other progressive families in Oak Park, were to play and learn with the Froebel Gifts.

In conventional terms, however, Wright had very little formal education as an architect. He completed just two semesters in engineering at the University of Wisconsin, while working in his professor's office practice, before he left to join the firm of J. Lynan Silsbee in Chicago. This was a post he obtained through a family connection, a strategic move that was to decide his future.

At the time, Chicago was in the midst of an unprecedented building boom following the fire of 1871, which almost entirely destroyed its downtown area. Wright managed to secure a position in the leading architectural firm of Adler and Sullivan, where he trained from 1888–93. Louis Sullivan was to become Wright's "Lieber Meister" and mentor, and his philosophy of architecture was to remain with Wright as a major influence throughout his life. In 1889, Sullivan was also to provide crucial financial support for his young apprentice in the form of a loan of $5,000. This enabled the 22 year old to begin building what was originally a modest six-room bungalow for his wife and growing family at Oak Park, where he began his experiments with organic architecture. Wright translated Sullivan's work from major public buildings—such as the Chicago Stock Exchange, with its inward looking, two-story trading room, which had an integrated decorative scheme based on organic forms and was naturally lit, to the vast and technologically advanced Auditorium building—and brought it to the private domain. The Adler and Sullivan practice was so busy with major public commissions, in what was fast becoming a showcase city, that domestic work was, in the main, entrusted to their chief draftsman, as Wright was soon to become, while the partners still retained overall supervision over more important commissions such as the Charnley Residence of 1891.

While Wright was working out his apprenticeship, he undertook several "bootleg" commissions he obtained on the side, which led eventually to his departure from the practice in 1893, the year of the World's Columbian Exposition, which brought 27 million visitors to the "White City" in Chicago during the course of the summer. By then Wright was part of an enlightened circle at the forefront of the city's development.

Wright's clients shared interests and ambitions with their architect that transcended the usual client/architect relationship. They, like him, were bringing up young families in new territory, and comfort and a quality of repose in the domestic space were seen as crucial. This extended to the design of furniture, glass, and the new technology of electrical lighting. The comfort factor was key in the extremes of temperature in Chicago and its environs, and, again, such features as the jutting eaves of the houses and the use of art glass to ensure privacy on suburban streets were evolved in response to this, with Wright using

his own home and showcase studio to demonstrate such innovations to his clients.

The quality of repose sought by Wright in the design of domestic interiors throughout his career is present in the very early domestic commissions, such as the William H. Winslow House. Clients such as Winslow required of their homes that they be all that their workplaces were not, a characteristic that is part of the architectural and design history of the late nineteenth century suburb in both America and Europe. The male domain of the workplace was reached by railway—Oak Park is ten miles west of Chicago and was well served by commuter lines in Wright's time—while the female domain of the home was conceived as a place apart: "the house beautiful." In addition, the wives of many of Wright's early clients were involved in the household reform movement in America, which had taken new impetus from the Nation Household Economics Association, founded by the women's congress at the Chicago World's Columbian Exposition of 1893.

Although the influence of Sullivan can be seen in Wright's early buildings, especially in the floriated forms of the glass designs, Wright was soon to move beyond Sullivan in both his use of new technologies and in his emphasis on the centrality of what he termed "a good plan." As far as Wright was concerned "a good plan (is)...the beginning and the end, because every good plan is organic...there is more beauty in a fine ground plan than in almost any of its ultimate consequences. In itself it will have the rhythms, masses and proportions of a good decoration if it is the organic plan for an organic building with individual style consistent with materials." It is this emphasis on consistency with materials that soon set Wright apart from his master, Sullivan. In a quintessential Sullivan interior such as that of the reconstructed trading room of the Chicago Stock Exchange, the design elements are interchangeable, whether they are for walls or glass: the stencil patterns used for the ceiling are nearly identical to the motifs of the skylights, irrespective of materials.

Wright followed the idea of "truth to materials," promulgated by William Morris and the Arts and Crafts Movement, even in such an early building as his own Home and Studio at Oak Park. Wright and his predecessors believed in the crucial importance of the integrity of materials, which included such time-honoured materials as glass, wood, and metal, used in their natural "honest" state. The leading English Arts and Crafts designer, Charles R. Ashbee, was to become a friend of Wright's, whose work he much admired.

Wright's early career coincided with radical advances in technology, in glass production for example, and he embraced each change as it came, incorporating it into his philosophy and practice of an organic architecture. Until 1883, plate glass had to be imported from Europe and was correspondingly expensive to use, while by the 1920s radical flat sheet methods made it possible for Wright to further open up the spaces of both public and private buildings to the world outside where appropriate.

Wright was to extend the use of the most humble materials to new and unexpected structures from early in his career. At Unity Temple in Oak Park, designed in 1905 and dedicated in 1908, Wright used concrete in his quest to destroy the box, a central tenet of his architectural philosophy, whether it was applied to a domestic dwelling or to a place of worship. At Unity Temple the concrete walls became screens, as they no longer had a supporting role, and their new function was enhanced and extended by a screen of windows above. This spectacular dissolution of the traditional post and lintel form of the cube was a radical concept, particularly when applied to a religious structure. Wright was the first to recognize the importance of his own work: "I had the beginning of a great thing, a great truth in architecture. Now architecture could be free." He was to extend the use of this new freedom in later public buildings using concrete, notably the Johnson Wax Administration building and the Solomon Guggenheim Museum, New York.

Wright shared a belief with such pioneers of modern design as William Morris that in the design of everyday objects such as chairs and tables, form should follow function and that the design of such objects should be an integrated part of the whole building. Indeed by 1901 when Wright published his plans for "A Home in a Prairie Town" in the February edition of the popular periodical *The Ladies' Home Journal*, which was to bring his work to the attention of a wide public, he declared a resounding belief in modernity, rejecting the "utter helplessness of old forms to satisfy new conditions" and praising the artist "who accepts, works and, sings as he works with the joy of the here and now."

The "here and now" were to remain central to Wright's philosophy, together with his long held belief that "A building can only be functional when integral with environment and so formed in the nature of materials according to purpose and method as to be a living entity." He put this into practice in the home and studio he built for himself and his family in the leafy suburb at Oak Park, Chicago, adapting and evolving it over a period of some 20 years. Oak Park became the forcing ground for many of Wright's radical ideas, and may be regarded as a species of laboratory in which Wright both experimented with his ideas and experienced their reality.

Part of this experimentation and experience was with the nature of materials and their true function and means of production. Unlike such nineteenth-century pioneers as Morris, Wright, together with many of his European and American contemporaries, could see the utility of machine production, which by the turn of the century was more generally regarded as a positive contribution to the quality of everyday life and the means by which a hitherto undreamed of range of goods could be brought within the range of ordinary people. Wright's friend, the leading English Arts and Crafts designer, Charles R. Ashbee, quoted Wright's emphatic espousal of the machine at their first meeting: "My God is Machinery; and the art of the future will be the expression of the individual artist through the thousand powers of the machine—the machine doing all those things that the individual workman cannot do. The creative artist is the man who controls all this and understands it."

Central to Wright's embrace of new technologies in the Chicago years was his interest in the Luxfer prism, for which he provided a design as early as 1894. His investment in the cutting edge of new technology provided him with the capital to build both the Studio and Library as additions to his home in Oak Park. Wright's clients at the time included several members of the Luxfer Prism Company's board

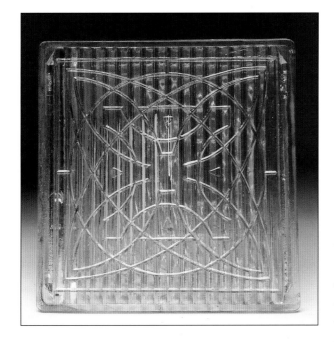

and the Company was very successful in supplying the burgeoning city of Chicago with the means to light storefronts and sidewalks before the widespread use of electric and neon lighting. The prisms, or more specifically tiles, used the principle of refraction to bend light into hitherto unlightable spaces, particularly those in deep courts and wells, or on narrow streets bordered by tall buildings. Thus concentrated, the light produced was invaluable for bringing daylight into factories, offices and homes. On the domestic front, the American Luxfer Prism company stated their claims for their electroglazing process (which) "means a revolution in the manufacture of art-leaded glass," as it "produced metal lines as narrow and accurate as if drawn with a ruling pen." Wright was to use the process from this period on. It is an essential feature of his art-glass designs, setting them apart from those of his contemporaries such as Lewis Comfort Tiffany. As will be seen, Wright was never to lose his interest in cutting-edge technology: the use of Pyrex tubes in the Johnson Wax Administration Building of 1936 to bring natural light into a huge, inward-looking working space is but one example in his later work.

Electroglazed art glass is a key feature of the Prairie Houses, which occupied Wright and his practice until his departure from Oak Park in 1909. The designs that emanated from Wright's studios were to transform domestic design and create new models for living both in the United States and abroad. Even as a young man, Wright realized the value of the dissemination of ideas in prestigious publications. The 1890s, which saw his building of grand houses for affluent clients also saw publication of his designs for "A small House with Lots of Room in

It." He kept himself well-informed on current movements throughout his life and placed his own work judiciously in American and European publications. The "Prairie Designs" received wide publicity in the so-called *Wasmuth Portfolio* published by Ernst Wasmuth in Germany in 1910. Much of the success of these designs lay in their "exotic" use of space and light, the "breaking of the box" and their sympathetic use of natural materials in an integrated organic design. Each of these features was in marked contrast to the constraints of the general run of domestic architecture of the time and its lack of integration with its spatial context.

Throughout the quintessential Prairie house, the Robie House (1908–10) in Chicago, for example, the design elements are integrated to an unprecedented degree, including Wright-designed built-in furniture and lighting fixtures, together with textiles that use the same design motifs as the window glass. The Prairie houses were distinguished by their custom-made designs. This attention to his clients' desires ran throughout Wright's career, from the affluence of the Prairie houses and the extravagance of the California textile block houses to the modest Usonians of his last years, a radical series of small houses that realized distinctive architectural design and the individuality of the owner, but at an economical price.

Despite the success of the Prairie houses, by 1909 Wright felt that he had reached an impasse in his life and work: "This absorbing, consuming phase of my experience as an architect ended about 1909...I was losing grip on my work and even interest in it. Abandoning his wife and family in Oak Park, he decamped with Mamah Borthwick Cheney, the wife of a client, and responded to an earlier invitation to go to Europe to assist in the publication of his designs in the highly influential *Wasmuth Portfolio*. On his return, a year later he began work on a hillside site near Spring Green, Wisconsin, where he had spent his childhood. He named the house, which quickly became a much more ambitious design, "Taliesin," a reference to his Welsh maternal roots; in Welsh, the word means "shining brow."

Up until this time, all Wright's commissions had been for urban or suburban sites. Here at the first Taliesin, the building could be designed

Above: Luxfer prism glass block. Wright patented around 40 Luxfer glass prism and plate designs. One of the most characteristic designs, this block, from 1897, was widely used to bring light into commercial buildings before the widespread use of electric light.

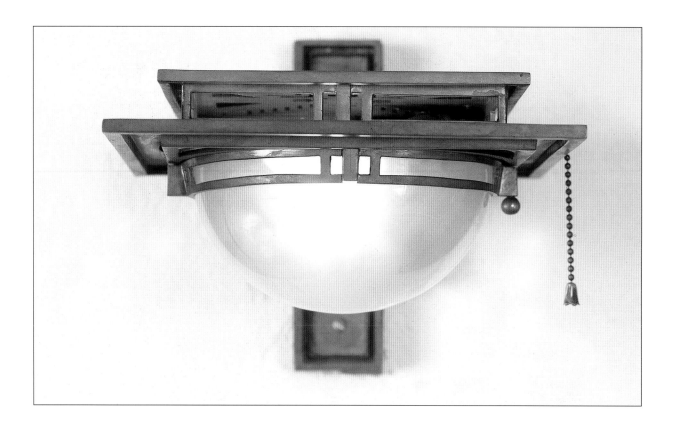

to take full advantage of the spectacular surrounding countryside and its place organically within it—"a broad shelter," in Wright's words, "seeking fellowship with its surroundings." Taliesin was remodelled over the years to suit the needs of what became a self-sufficient working community that incorporated a farm and other functional buildings. The windows in this rural setting were designed as long, uninterrupted bands of glass, protected by steep eaves, which enabled them to be left opened "to the breezes of summer and become like an open camp if need be." The complex stretched gradually across the hill, eventually incorporating some 3,000 acres.

After the tragic fire and loss of his new family at Taliesin in 1914, Wright's life and work were never the same again.

His work on the Imperial Hotel in Tokyo occupied him from 1916 to 1922 and here he was able to incorporate architectural and design elements drawn from a culture he had long admired, not only into the

design of the building itself but into the many artefacts that formed so crucial a part of the design as a whole, from furniture to ceramics and lighting. The Japanese influence was to remain with Wright for the rest of his career, while the project was crucial to his professional reputation in these years, especially after the great Kanto earthquake of 1923, when it survived more or less intact while buildings around it were flattened to the ground. This was partly due to its steel structural reinforcement—what Wright was to define as "the ability to push and pull on a building." The evolution of this technique, and the use of concrete, which made it possible, was to stand Wright in good stead for another area of great natural turbulence in his native country.

Wright's new clients in California required radically different solutions from their architect, as did the sites and climatic conditions he was now called on to work with. Wright worked on five major commissions for houses in the Los Angeles area while simultaneously

Above: Frederick C. Robie House, Chicago, Ill. Spherical wall-light fixture, part of the "grammar" of geometric forms used throughout the house. The details of the bronze fitment are particularly fine, extending to the light pull.

completing the Imperial Hotel. Each was radical in both its use of space, light, and an integrated design scheme. Each was built of textured concrete block, a material he had used in the construction of several public commissions, including the current work on the Imperial Hotel.

The innovative possibilities of concrete were used throughout the construction and decorative elements of the 200-square-foot spectacular entertainment center, the Midway Gardens in Chicago, which opened in 1914 with "as brilliant a social event as Chicago ever knew…the architectural scheme of color, form, light and sound, came alive," as Wright wrote in *An Autobiography*. Surviving photographs of the complex, and indeed, some of the remaining sculptural fragments, demonstrate the extraordinary richness of the Gardens and their ornamentation. In the Midway Gardens, Wright realized a fantasy that found a response, albeit short-lived, in the public. "Chicago marveled, acclaimed, approved. And Chicago went back and did the same again and again and again. It was 'Egyptian' to many, Maya to some, Japanese to others. Strange to all."

True to the spirit of the age "it awaked a sense of mystery and romance in them all to which each responded with what he had in him to give." However, the turbulent times ahead were unpropitious for such a fantastical place of entertainment; the outbreak of World War I closely followed its opening, and the complex was finally demolished in 1929.

This short-lived realization of a fantasy for public consumption was to be succeeded by the Californian textile block houses, which he described as "Romanza," a term that can be perceived as the realization of myth or fantasy. The houses are "dream houses" that draw on the particular spirit of the place in all their design elements. A major factor in Wright's attraction to Southern California was his sense that the region was a desert that could be changed out of all recognition, and that here, both historically and symbolically, the land was related to pre-Columbian culture. The motifs and structures employed in the Barnsdall and other Californian houses, most notably perhaps in the Ennis House, are linked with Wright's continuing quest for "primitive" and non-Western sources as an inspirational force in his work. The

Right: The loggia of the Mabel and Charles Ennis House, Los Angeles, California. The dramatic loggia runs almost the entire length of the grandest of Wright's textile-block designs, linking the rooms and opening onto terraces at either side.

Barnsdall House ("Hollyhock House"), which was conceived for the most part in Japan, while Wright was working on the complexities of the Imperial Hotel project, combines an eclectic mix of influences, seen at its most complex in the living room. The skylights are of a form he was currently using in the Imperial Hotel design and the central feature of the entire house, the "sacred hearth," which Wright always considered of paramount importance, is reflected in a shallow pool. The distinctive overmantel bears a carved relief purportedly of Aline Barnsdall seated upon a throne, as a freely interpreted abstract representation of Amerindian myth, in one of Wright's most extraordinary flights of fantasy.

In California, the textile block construction system created its own spatial lexicon, taking its motif from the block itself, and this is followed through both internally and externally, providing Wright with hitherto undreamed of possibilities of manipulating light and shadow. The perforated blocks used at the Storer House, for example, permit filtered light to create exciting shadow patterns in the interior spaces, while identical blocks, lit from within, provide dramatic emphasis to the exterior elevations at night.

The textile block houses were equally remarkable for their fully integrated designs that follow through a chosen motif, such as the hollyhock at the Aline Barnsdall House. The client's favorite flower is used in abstract form throughout the house, from the stylized flower motifs on the exterior to the chairs and light fixtures that incorporate the flower into their design. Perhaps most striking of all are the abstract hollyhock motifs used for the design of the art glass. The colors used in it are all derived from hollyhock tones, varying in hue from pale lavender to dark purple.

In the last decade of his life, in *The Natural House*, Wright declared that "the best way to light a house is "God's way—the natural way, as nearly as possible in the daytime and at night as nearly like the day as may be, or better." He had first used a wooden light screen above the dining table in the remodeling of his own house and studio at Oak Park. At that time Wright was fascinated by the new possibilities of using electric lighting in the home, and devised an ingenious grille with a pattern of circular motifs to convey the effect of light falling through leaves. Originally light bulbs were installed behind rice paper to diffuse the light behind the screen and illuminate the family dinner table. This device was to be developed in increasingly complex forms during his Californian period. The living room skylight in the Barnsdall House, for example, is formed of a rectilinear wooden frame interspersed with long lines of tiny geometric patterned glass and clear glass that give a lightness of feeling and structure new to Wright's work. Other textile block houses employed familiar Wrightian style and design devices in radically changed forms.

In the Freeman House, for example, the use of repeating abstract and stylized tulip-like forms in the perforated light blocks is particularly notable. The apertures afford privacy, while throwing unique shadows throughout the house, an effect to be seen at its most dramatic in the clerestory windows of the living room. These serve to emphasize a contrast particularly dear to Wright's heart throughout his career, the contrast of the shelter-like forms of the interior with the panoramic views that are seen through the plate glass windows of the city of Los Angeles below.

The consistency of Wright's use of what he termed "light screens" in the widest sense and in a variety of materials is a remarkable feature of his career. A recessed perforated skylight to add interesting top lighting comparable to that used in the California houses may be said to have a precedent in the playroom at Oak Park and similar devices are used in other houses of the period, while the dramatic possibilities of clerestory windows in a domestic setting, used to such dramatic effect in the textile block houses is adapted to wood-panel cut-outs and screens in the embellishment of the various forms of the moderately priced Usonian houses of the 1930s and 1940s.

One of the many extraordinary features of Wright's style and design is his ability to adjust his work to changing circumstances, a characteristic that is nowhere clearer than in his remarkable final phase of creativity, which brought him and his work back into the architectural limelight and to the center of public attention, further fostered by his lecture tours, television appearances, and many publications.

Left: The Solomon Guggenheim Museum, New York. View of the hemispherical dome and spiral ramp and the skylights or "rifts" that run the entire length of the ramp on its outer edge, enclosing a system of incandescent tubes, which enhance the natural light.

Wright's capacity for reinventing himself and responding to changing social and economic climates is a marked and constant feature of his long and productive career. The last quarter century of his extraordinarily creative life included such landmarks as the setting up of the Taliesin Fellowship and Taliesin West, which ensured the training and productivity of the next generation of Wright-trained architects, the building of the Marin County Administration complex and the Solomon Guggenheim Museum, New York. In the domestic domain his major achievements were Fallingwater and the Usonian houses, both regarded as mold-breaking concepts in their time and as key contributions to the history of Western architecture ever since. In particular, the Usonian designs were seen to address the real needs of middle-income families in times of unprecedented economic uncertainty. The fact that Wright was able to realize the houses so speedily within a strict budget, and without the seemingly idiosyncratic and exotic qualities that had distinguished his domestic work for wealthier clients, further ensured their success.

By January 1938, a portrait of Wright featured on the front cover of *Time* with the heading "Frank Lloyd Wright, Usonian Architect," and a long illustrated article detailed recent projects, including the Johnson Wax Building, the Johnson Residence, "Wingspread," Fallingwater, and the Jacobs house by an architect thought by many to be a spent force at 63. Within a year Wright was to further publicize his work with a lecture series, later published as "An Organic Architecture: the Architecture of Democracy," which had a particular resonance in 1939, just before World War II began.

The first Usonian to be built, the Jacobs House demonstrates several key Wrightian concepts that it shares with the earlier Prairie Houses and Fallingwater. The most significant of these is its integration with its site. Fallingwater, famously, is cantilevered over a waterfall on a spectacular site at Mill Run, Pennsylvania, and Wright's aim of working with nature is similarly apparent in the modest Jacobs House.

Wright's long held belief that in the interests of regarding the whole interior space as an integral unit, doors, windows, and other openings should be conceived as part of an integrated structure, and that all necessary fittings, and indeed as much furniture as was practicable, should be built-in, to give his much-prized qualities of "simplicity and repose," which is seen particularly clearly in his last domestic designs. This is made more remarkable by the necessity, in the interests of economy, to devise a technologically radical construction and assembly process for the early Usonians that satisfied both economic and aesthetic considerations—some were indeed part-worked on by their

Right: Sidney Bazett (Bazett-Frank) House, Hillsborough, California. Living room with dining area and hearth. The dining area is served by the workspace (which is lit by a skylight) behind the hearth.

owners. The fixtures and fittings offered opportunities for creative construction, while sacrificing nothing in their attention to detail and the lifestyle of their owners. Wright's aim was to provide "modest-cost houses" while declaring his belief that "there is nothing more interesting or more important in this world today than trying to put into the houses in which our typical best citizens live something of the quality of a genuine work of art."

Both Wright's continuing modernity and his distance from his peers may be seen in the style and design of his houses, particularly in the way he responded to his clients needs, bringing a humanizing quality to contemporary domestic design. This can be observed throughout his career, and is nowhere more apparent than in his response to the Depression years in providing practical housing at modest cost. The quintessential Prairie house, the Robie House, remarkable for its integrated custom-built design, was built at a cost of $35,000 in 1909. The Herbert and Katherine Jacobs House, completed in 1937 cost $5,500, which included the architect's fee, combining, as did many of the early Usonians, "the magic of Wright's name...with a price tag that made it all seem possible," in the words of its first owners.

Wright's remarkable consistency of style and design may also be seen in the Usonians, together with evidence of his extraordinary ability to adapt to changing social and economic circumstance. For example the patterned shadows cast through the clerestory windows were remembered long after as part of the unique atmosphere of the Usonian interior by those who had lived in them. Wright had used the device before in the pierced glazed patterns of the Californian textile block houses, while floor to ceiling windows in the rooms requiring less privacy had formed part of his early designs, providing the key component of a glass screen onto nature while bringing the outside inside. Marked horizontality of the design of a building and its integration with its site is another key feature of his work, as apparent in the Prairie houses as in his last works, from the Usonian houses to Marin County Civic Center.

In a radical new departure, four years before his death, Wright was to design furniture and furnishings for a hitherto untapped market, including designs for textiles and even wallpapers, which had not previously featured in his work. His life-long principles of an organic architectural and design unity meant that Wright had always designed furnishings in terms of specific buildings, even the furniture for the Johnson and Price Tower buildings, although produced in large numbers, was entirely site-specific, and the needs of the individual client were paramount. However, from 1955, designs for the average consumer were produced commercially, bringing them within the reach of the general public.

Throughout his long career Wright's response to the challenges of a changing world was one of extraordinary creativity in both his public and private buildings. His first commissions were for houses, and while the designs that made his name, the Prairie houses, were extraordinarily radical in their time, they were built for affluent clients with kitchen, living and dining rooms designed as separate spaces, however open in aspect. His later designs continued to "break the box" of the conventional domestic interior while meeting the needs of affluent clients. In contrast, his final houses responded to seismic changes in family life, especially to the changing status of women. As Wright himself explained in 1948, in the modern, servantless household, the woman of the house became its central figure. The style and design of the Usonian house makes this possible. In moving the kitchen to the center of the house, to become its hub and renaming it a "workspace," Wright explained that "family processes are conveniently centralized," while the woman of the house, instead of being "a kitchen mechanic behind closed doors," became its central figure a "hostess officio." With the kitchen workspace as the hub of the household, the new greater informality of domestic life could be accommodated, eliminating the need for a formal dining room, which had once been regarded as a separate space and a key element in both form and furnishings of Wright's early success. In losing its function it had become an anachronism.

Yet again Wright had put into practice his belief in modernity, first expressed in 1901 when he had declared the "utter helplessness of old forms to satisfy new conditions" and praised the artist who, "works with the joy of the here and now."

FURNITURE

FRANK LLOYD WRIGHT HOME AND STUDIO, FREDERICK C. ROBIE HOUSE, POPE LEIGHEY HOUSE, S.C. JOHNSON WAX ADMINISTRATION BUILDING, FALLINGWATER, AND THE KAUFMANN OFFICE.

For Wright, from the very beginning

of his career as an architect, each piece of furniture was considered to be an integral part of an organic whole. Each chair, each table had its own nature, yet was part of a site-specific structure and was part of its unique vocabulary. In the breaking of the box of conventional spaces, so crucial to Wright's design and style ethos, and the dissolving of the barriers between the interior and the exterior, Wright was concerned to bring nature inside the domestic interior. The use of glass was an essential part of this scheme, helping to dissolve the barriers between inside and outside in order to create the "vista without" and the "vista within." The use of wood as the major material for his interiors, quite literally brought nature inside. Wood was used in huge quantities in Wright's interiors, from the earliest buildings in Oak Park, where, appropriately, oak was the favored wood for both furniture and house trim, to the final designs of his career, where redwood or cypress was usually used throughout the interior and the exterior design.

Wright was remarkably consistent in his use of and respect for wood. His early custom-made and built-in furniture was made in either Chicago or Milwaukee from the ample supplies of oak to be found in the forests of Wisconsin that fed the thriving furniture industry at the turn of the nineteenth century.

Above right: Chair and built-in seating at Taliesin West, Scottsdale, Arizona. The celebrated plywood chairs, first used at Taliesin West, resemble folded origami forms.

Right: Taliesin West, Scottsdale, Arizona. The Garden Room. Taliesin West is based on a triangular module. Boulders from the surrounding landscape are set into the rubble walls and hearth and the space is lit by translucent skylights.

Right: Taliesin West, Scottsdale, Arizona. Garden Room from the hearth. The key motif of the entire complex is the triangle, drawn from the nature of the site itself and its surrounding mountain ranges.

Built-in furniture was an important factor in realizing the fully integrated organic interior and Wright also saw these fitments as a means of controlling the client's use of discordant and inappropriate furniture, particularly as furniture design of the period was extraordinarily ornate. As early as 1894 Wright had stated his ideal: "The most truly satisfactory apartments are those in which most or all the furniture is built in as part of the original scheme considering the whole as an integral unit." He despaired however of finding suitable furnishings for such interiors: "Simple things at that time in any industrial field were nowhere at hand. A piece of wood without a molding was an anomaly: a plain wooden slat instead of a turned baluster a joke…plain fabrics for hangings or floor covering were nowhere to be found in stock."

Wright aimed for an effect of what he described as "distinguished simplicity" in his organic designs, using geometric forms that eliminated all excess ornamentation, yet were subtle and sophisticated in appearance, as distinct from the contemporary Mission furniture of the designers Stickley and Roycroft, which he termed "plain as a barn door." This "truly simple" early furniture depends on harmonious proportions forming a symmetrical and functional whole without the use of extensive joinery or carved ornamentation.

The forms of Wright's early furniture were clearly directed by a combination of design influences: crucial among these appears to have been the influence of Japanese prints, which Wright had been collecting for some time and which continued to be a seminal influence on his work throughout his life. Wright did not visit Japan until 1905, but he had studied the refined proportions and use of natural materials in representations of houses in Japanese prints long before this. The contemplative and spiritual nature of Japanese design was also attractive to him and the prints conveyed the fact that, not only were the spaces in the characteristic Japanese interior dissolved by the use of screens, but that much of the furniture was built-in and that the central focus of the home was the hearth. Even in his earliest work, Wright set about synthesizing this oriental view of harmonizing the modern home with nature and that of the Arts and Crafts ideals imported from Britain, which were another seminal early influence on his work. William

Above right: George Barton House, Buffalo, New York. Dining room cabinet. The built-in china cabinet with art-glass doors is illuminated from above and shares the dominant abstracted plant form motifs seen in the windows of the house.

Right: Bookcase from the George Stockman House, Mason City, Iowa. The rectilinear banding of this glass-fronted bookcase is echoed in the oak paneling and mirror above.

Morris and his followers had placed high importance on the total design of furnishings and building, together with its setting and the nature of materials. However, Wright, together with many of his European and American contemporaries, differed from Morris and other nineteenth-century pioneers in that they could see the utility of machine production, which by the turn of the century was more generally regarded as a positive contribution to the quality of everyday life and the means by which a hitherto undreamed of range of goods could be brought within the range of ordinary people.

In furniture, for example, the new forms of woodworking machinery were able to manufacture domestic furniture relatively inexpensively and quickly. In March 1901, Wright, who was a charter member of the aestheticising reform movement, the Chicago Arts and Crafts Society, delivered a statement of his own progressive position in a lecture to the Society, "The Art and Craft of the Machine," in which he stated "William Morris pleaded well for simplicity as the basis of all true art. Let us understand the significance to art of the word—simplicity—for it is vital to the art of the machine." Wright acknowledged that "the machine is here to stay" and that this would not only influence design and architecture, as in, for example, simple, straight lines of cut wood for furniture rather than elaborate curved shapes, but that the machine would help bring about a new fabric of society.

Wright was later to clarify his position on mechanization to his friend, the English Arts and Crafts designer, Charles R. Ashbee: "My God," he explained, is "Machinery; and the art of the future will be the expression of the individual artist through the thousand powers of the machine…The creative artist is the man who controls all this and understands it."

Wright's work of the Oak Park years contains many references to Arts and Crafts influence, most clearly seen in his early use of a built-in feature so characteristic of that movement, the fire-side inglenook. The focal point of the living room in his own house at Oak Park, which was building from 1889 to 1895, is a brick-built hearth within a cozy inglenook. The idea of what Wright was to term "the sacred hearth" as the heart of the home and of family life, is seen in its clearest form here,

complete with its carved Arts and Crafts inspired text "Truth is Life" (the second motto "Good Friend, around these hearth-stones speak no evil word of any creature" was added at a later date), which emphasizes the special status of the space. The inglenook space could have floor-length curtains drawn around it to ensure greater privacy. Such focal points were to feature strongly throughout his domestic work, all as variations on the idea of the "sacred hearth" and expressed on the exterior of the building by a prominent chimney.

Wright's early "bootleg" commission for the George Blossom house of 1892, which was one of several exercises by Wright in an historical mode of the period, was built in New England Colonial Revival style with symmetrical front, and clapboard siding. The interior is remarkable for the inclusion of an inglenook with fitted seating and cupboards above the fireplace, which is faced with olive tiles and

Above: George Blossom House, Chicago, Illinois. Entrance front. The classicism of the façade is enhanced by Wright's choice of Ionic columns, the most elegant of the orders of classical architecture, to form an exercise in the newly fashionable New England Colonial style.

Above left: George Blossom House, Chicago, Illinois. The dining room opens out of the living room and is framed within an arch to provide a "vista within." The formality of the design, with the windows set in a curve, also evokes the New England Colonial style.

framed from the anteroom within a double-banded wooden archway, providing a "vista within." The house is also fitted with built-in window seats and a buffet. From such early examples, it is easy to trace the development of the "sacred hearth" in Wright's work through the twentieth century, from the dramatic central feature of "Wingspread" to its use in the Usonian Houses of Wright's final years.

This widespread use of built-ins was a cornerstone of Wright's idea of an organic architecture. As he explained in 1910:

> In Organic Architecture then, it is quite impossible to consider the building as one thing, its furnishings another and its setting and environment still another. The Spirit in which these buildings are conceived sees all these together at work as one thing. All are to be studiously foreseen and provided for in the nature of the structure. Incorporated (or excluded) are lighting, heating and ventilation. The very chairs and tables, cabinets, and even musical instruments, where practicable, are of the building itself, never fixtures upon it. No appliances or fixtures are admitted as such where circumstances permit the full development of the organic character of the building scheme.

At the Home and Studio, built-in fixtures are a major feature of the design, particularly in the additions to the original structure, which were made in 1895. The extended space of the dining room, for example, was Wright's first fully worked out total environment, incorporating the architecture and built-in fitments, free standing furniture, art glass, lighting fixtures, and ornamentation into an integrated whole. The room attracted a great deal of attention at the time, and was reviewed in 1899 for the magazine House Beautiful.

The reviewer was particularly impressed by "its simplicity—no rugs, no curtains and only the necessary furniture, which, however is in perfect harmony with the room…The oak woodwork, which is carried round the room to the height of the window-sills, is designed to emphasize the horizontal line, a very wise thought in a small room."

The barrel-vaulted playroom for Wright's growing family was provided with some of the most imaginative built-in furniture in the entire complex. A full range of shelves and storage, together with glass-fronted toy-cupboards and a raised seating area provided a child-centered

space, which is scaled accordingly. Indeed, the windows are at the height of a child and adults have to stoop to look out of them. The room is designed for play and learning, accommodating Catherine Tobin Wright's work with the Froebel blocks—which had been so influential a factor in her husband's childhood, and which she and other progressive mothers continued to use as a teaching method with their own children—as well as the many entertainments devised by the six Wright children, which could be watched from the purpose-built raised seating. Throughout his life, childhood had an almost mystic connotation for Wright. In 1932 he observed that "Human beings are really childlike, in the best sense, when directly appealed to by very simple, strong forms and pure, bright color." Wright's son, John Lloyd Wright, has recalled his father's particular fascination for brightly colored gas-filled balloons in the playroom at Oak Park, which might perhaps be seen reflected in the different levels at which the globular glass fitments are hung there.

The working environment of the Studio complex was provided with a finely crafted range of built-in furniture to accommodate the busy practice in what was both a fitting working environment and a showcase for clients. Other Oak Park and River Forest commissions of the time also had built-in shelves and cupboards as an essential part of the design. In the Warren McArthur House of 1892, Wright took the

Right: Warren McArthur House, Chicago, Illinois. Built-in sideboard and buffet of dining room. Wright was commissioned in 1902 to design the elaborate dining room fixtures and matching doors as an embellishment to the original house.

Right: Warren McArthur House, Chicago, Illinois. Detail of sideboard and buffet in the dining room. The wall length fixture is made from Californian oak and the art-glass doors share the same arrow-headed design as the dining room doors.

Below left: Lowell and Agnes
Walter House ("Cedar Rock"),
Quasqueton, Iowa. Garden room.
Wright designed much of the built-in
and free-standing furniture. Walnut is
used throughout and the specially
designed seating can be moved to
form different combinations.

opportunity in 1902 of remodeling the dining room with elaborate oak fixtures, including an impressive built-in buffet with art-glass doors in a distinctive geometric design that is echoed in the double doors to the room.

Built-in furniture continues to feature in the Prairie and textile block houses, although pride of place is given to the free-standing furniture distinctively designed for each house. The lessons learned in his early work in terms of what could be done with built in furniture, however, receive their most remarkable flowering in the low-cost Usonian houses in the last decades of Wright's career.

Wright's capacity for reinventing himself and responding to changing social and economic climates is a marked and constant feature of his long and productive career. His response to the need for low-cost, modern housing, which followed the stock market crash of 1929 and the Great Depression, was to apply his lifelong principles of organic architecture to what he was to term the Usonian house. The Usonian

designs brought Wright popularity because they were seen to address the real needs of middle-income families in times of unprecedented economic uncertainty. The fact that Wright was able to realize the house so speedily within a strict budget, and without the seemingly idiosyncratic and exotic qualities that had distinguished his domestic work for wealthier clients, further ensured their success. In simplifying the design, by eliminating all that was not essential, Wright devised a technologically radical construction and assembly process for the early Usonians that satisfied both economic and aesthetic considerations. Each house rested on a concrete platform with heating pipes cast into it to provide gravity heating throughout the space, eliminating the need for radiators, a particular bugbear for Wright. Most of the furniture was built in to the walls and was uncomplicated enough in design to be constructed on the site by local labor or the owners.

In Wright's drawings and in the houses themselves, a unit module and geometrical grid were used, which made it possible for the early

Below right: Lowell and Agnes
Walter House ("Cedar Rock"),
Quasqueton, Iowa. Bedroom. Built-in
shelves and storage are constructed
to the same module and are made of
the same material as the paneling,
producing a streamlined, organic
space.

Usonians to be built by local contractors, or in some cases by the owners themselves, using standard materials in standard sizes, working to
the specific module of the house, whether it be rectangular, hexagonal,
or other geometric form, which was often inscribed in the concrete
floor. The board-and-batten construction, ready-manufactured from
pine (grained cypress was often used in later houses), which served as
both exterior and interior finish, eliminated the necessity for interior
wall coverings.

However the built-in furniture, which proved so distinctive a feature of each individual Usonian, was far from standardized. Clients were
asked to supply a wants-list for their houses, with specifications for the
cupboards and shelving appropriate to their lifestyle. Thus, each
Usonian was adapted to the wishes of its owner, whether it was to
provide a living room space with the acoustic and seating requirements
for performing chamber music, or, in the case of the Goetsch-Winckler
House, storage for home preserved produce in cupboards that were
easily accessible to an owner who was five foot two.

The interiors of the Usonian houses are remarkable for their simplicity and integral design and decoration. All superfluous free-standing
furniture is eliminated and shelves and storage are constructed to the
same module, and often of the same materials as the house as a whole,
which helps in the achievement of a remarkable unity of form.

However, the fact that the disposition of the interior space and the
fixtures within it were determined allowed very little flexibility in the
accumulation of objects. Wright's attention to detail remained as constant as it had been throughout his career, and the owners of the
Goetsch-Winckler House recalled removing a Bauhaus-designed chair
when Wright was due to visit and replacing it after he had gone, as they
feared their architect's scorn at such an intrusion from those he
termed "the Bauhaus boys" into one of his houses.

Wright's control of the free-standing elements of his designs had
always been a key part of his notion of an organic architecture. In devel-
oping the use of built-in cabinets, seating, and bookcases in his early
designs he was both adopting a standard practice in Victorian house
design and ensuring that the constituent parts of the interior had

appeared to grow naturally. He was also ensuring that his clients were
not able to use furniture that was out of keeping with the interior, and
that might put the wholeness of the organic design at risk. For Wright
each separate chair is part of the overall matrix of style and design and
helps determine the use of space within it. A case in point is his design
for the famous high-back dining chair, which exists in several variants,
most famously perhaps in the set designed for the dining room at his
own house at Oak Park. The horizontality of the design of the room,
emphasized by the lines of the oak paneling and the banded design of
the art-glass windows is offset by the verticality of the eight tall high-
backed chairs. More elaborate in form than later models, the chairs had
a form of "twisted spindle" in their backs, soon to be replaced by vertical slats as the design evolved. The principle of enclosure and intima-
cy around the family dining table was maintained in later designs and
determined the special status of the space for the rituals of family

Above: Aline Barnsdall
("Hollyhock") House, Los Angeles,
California. Dining room table and
chairs. The high-backed upholstered
chairs and pedestal table are
decorated with the hollyhock, the
dominant motif of the house.

Right: Aline Barnsdall ("Hollyhock") House, Los Angeles, California. Side table, skylight and carpet. The hollyhock, the dominant motif of the Barnsdall House is woven into the carpet design, echoing the skylight above.

meals. The definition of an eating area within the larger space, by the screen-like effect of the chair-backs, is developed in later designs in larger spaces, such as those for the "Hollyhock House" in California.

At Oak Park, where Wright's growing family was eventually to number six children, the handsome oak table was extendable by means of sliding supports and additional leaves when needed for guests. When not in use, a long woven runner was used to emphasize its horizontality. To a modern eye the chairs look exceedingly uncomfortable, especially given the length and complexity of late nineteenth-century meals, and Wright was later to admit that his early approach to chair design was from a cultural and social viewpoint, rather than one of comfort. The strong vertical elements of the Oak Park chairs were to be developed for clients' furniture during the Oak Park years. The slatted chairs were designed before 1897, when they were photographed for an article in *House Beautiful*. The use of vertical slats as a decorative and screening device probably derives from Japanese design and had been used by British Arts and Crafts designers in the 1890s. Wright developed and simplified the geometry of the original designs, eliminating, for example, the circular finials that form such a distinctive motif on the original design.

When Wright first began designing custom-made furniture for his growing roster of clients in the Chicago area in the 1890s, Chicago had overtaken Grand Rapids as a leading center for furniture manufacture, and was advanced technologically, although craftsman skills were needed to produce the high quality bespoke furniture Wright demanded for his radically new designs. Wright was fortunate in the skills of the furniture making craftsmen he commissioned to execute his unadorned designs, especially as advances in technological processes made it easier to add traditional ornament in a style that found favor elsewhere.

It is difficult to put a precise date on much of Wright's furniture from the beginning of his career, especially as, in the very nature of an organic interior, furniture could be added over the years, and for Wright and his clients the design of a building was a continuous process. Wright often returned to make changes to his designs, as in that of the Warren MacArthur House, which was originally one of Wright's so-called "boot-leg" designs, built while Wright was apprenticed to Louis Sullivan and Jankel Adler's architectural practice. Very few of Wright's early clients could afford to furnish their houses completely from the beginning of their construction, and Wright was to return to the MacArthur commission ten years later to remodel the dining

Above left: Aline Barnsdall ("Hollyhock") House, Los Angeles, California. Detail of dining room paneling and windows. The paired casement windows are set in the extensive areas of paneling and are here seen against the light, revealing the stylized hollyhock motifs of the caming.

Above: Aline Barnsdall ("Hollyhock") House. Living room, looking toward the hearth. The massive sofa fixture, with its built-in lamp fitments and angled tables is unique in Wright's work.

Above: Zimmerman House, Manchester, New Hampshire. The quartet music stand and matching stools are copies of those at Taliesin. The stand is functional as well as decorative and could be illuminated from within.

room, providing it with furniture and the built-in sideboard fixture, which represents a pivotal point in Wright's use of art-glass.

The problem of tracing a precise chronology of Wright's furniture is particularly apparent in the case of chair design. Wright continued to use the high-backed design of dining chair in various forms throughout his career, although the slatted backs were gradually to give way to solid backs, which were almost certainly easier to manufacture and less expensive to produce. Dining chair design has traditionally favored high-backs, which demand a particularly straight-backed posture appropriate to formal dining. Wright was well aware of the criticism of lack of comfort leveled at his high-backed chairs, and in later years was to blame the social and cultural need for people to eat in what he termed a "folded" position, which he considered to be against nature. Wright admired the designs of some of his European contemporaries, which he would have known through such publications as *The International Studio* citing: "The Mackintoshes of Scotland; restless European Protestants

also—van de Velde of Holland... Adolph Loos and Otto Wagner of Vienna." The famous high-backed chairs of Charles Rennie Mackintosh bear an obvious similarity to Wright's designs. Mackintosh was an uncategorizable designer whose rectilinear style and abstract forms for decoration, allied to the functionality of his use of materials in such landmark buildings as the Glasgow School of Art and Miss Cranston's "tea-rooms" in that city, were exactly contemporary with Wright's work on his early houses.

Another British influence seems to have acted on Wright as stimulus for his early armchair designs. *The Studio* in 1894 reproduced the design of a tapestry by Edward Burne-Jones. Woven in the tapestry workshops of William Morris, it was one of a series of large tapestries from the "Holy Grail" series, representing "The Summons" to the medieval knights of King Arthur's Round Table. The knights are seated in simple, wooden chairs of austere design and pure shapes, with a rectangular-backed slatted chair and two barrel-shaped chairs with slatted backs turned toward the viewer, which may well have influenced Wright in his early armchair designs. However, the most radical of Wright's armchair designs, that of a cuboid form of chair, that appears in photographs of his own house and studio and dates from 1895, is of uncompromising severity, and appears to be influenced by the Froebel Gifts of his childhood, which reduced natural forms to their basic geometry. Variants on this chair were to appear in commissions throughout the Prairie years. Those from the Dana-Thomas House are perhaps the most famous. The two armchairs have spindle backs and are made of oak with upholstery. Each of the chairs has a spindle back and side, and each side has nine spindles. There is a variant on the spindle design elsewhere in the house, which has five sides rather than three, each with multiple spindles.

The square form of arm chair design reappears, subtly altered, throughout the Prairie years, often with upholstered backs, as well as seats, as in the chairs to be seen in the reconstructed living room of the Francis Little House in the Metropolitan Museum of Art, New York.

Another Prairie house, that for Darwin D. Martin is particularly well documented in terms of furniture design. Wright appears to have

introduced circular and semi-circular forms in the armchair designs for the house, which mark a change in terms of both refined craftsmanship and comfort from Wright's other furniture of the time. The joinery of the chairs is particularly elegant and the curved arms and back were infinitely more comfortable than the customary rectilinear arms and back; some eight armchairs were originally designed for use in different rooms throughout the Martin House. Originally upholstered in dark leather, this curved design was to have a longer life than other furniture of the same period. Wright was to revisit the Martin House in Buffalo, New York, some 30 years after it was built and saw the possibilities of reviving the form for very different times. Updated versions can be seen at Taliesin North and, especially finely crafted at the Herbert F. Johnson House ("Wingspread") in Racine, Wisconsin. In general, Wright's designs for armchairs evolved in terms of greater comfort and a more frequent use of upholstery.

The dining tables of the Oak Park years were also constructed from oak, massive in form with a substantial top and strong, square legs. The earliest recorded example is that in the dining room at the Home and Studio at Oak Park. Early photographs and drawings record the presence of wooden lamp standards at all four corners, which could also hold flowers, at the Robie House and other grand Prairie designs of the period, but these were abandoned as impractical, given the problems of electric lighting at that time. The basic form of dining table, which could be extended to accommodate guests, was to occupy Wright at different periods in his life. Identical tables were designed for the Dana-Thomas House, for example, which could be put together to accommodate the grand dinners given by the society hostess. The tables could also accommodate further seating if necessary as they had sliding supports for extra leaves. As the lifestyle of the family changed in the new century, Wright eliminated the dining room as a separate space altogether, incorporating an eating space for the family in the living room area. Such California textile block houses as the "Hollyhock House" still contain a variant on the characteristic form of the Wright dining table, complete with high-backed chairs. In contrast, "Wingspread" had a dining table that could be stored in the kitchen

Above left: Susan Lawrence Dana (Dana-Thomas) House. Living Hall Inglenook and oak settles. Wright designed the furnishings of the entire space, from the massive high-back settles to the firescreen and firedogs and even the tall Teco vase with its sumac flower decoration.

Left: Lowell and Agnes Walter House ("Cedar Rock"). The spacious garden room is provided with extensive built-in waxed walnut storage and modular seating which can be used to form different units.

when required, while the Usonian houses had a multi-purpose table that could be used for several family activities.

Wright had always designed tables for purposes other than dining. Notable among these are the print viewing tables designed for the Dana-Thomas House, and, later, for the Francis Little House in Wayzata, Minnesota. The oak tables were especially designed for the viewing of Japanese prints, which Wright collected and which became a seminal influence on his work. Several of his clients also collected prints and the viewing of them, in the case of the Dana-Thomas House, was a pleasurable activity for family and guests. Two of the tables remain in the Studio. The tops of the tables are hinged in the center so that they can be folded in an upright position and stored flat in a specially fitted section between the two posts when not in use. The tables are of an elegant, rectilinear design, and the four, gate-leg supports, like the top

posts, are spindled. The gate-leg posts could also be folded flat into the center, making a functional piece of furniture that was elegant and space-saving even when not in use.

Wright's work for the Dana-Thomas House also included special free-standing furniture designs, such as the splendid high-backed settle, with shelves at the back, which stands near the stairwell, and a music cabinet, which stands near one of the print tables, and may, by reason of its relatively clumsy design, have been the work of his studio.

After the triumphs of such Prairie houses as the Robie House, perhaps the most elegant and integrated of all Wright's designs, the California textile block houses required very different solutions in terms of furniture. There are, however, affinities with earlier designs. The "Hollyhock House" furniture has recognizable similarities to his earlier work, not least in the proportions of the dining chairs.

Right: Susan Lawrence Dana (Dana-Thomas) House, Springfield, Illinois. Living room bay looking southeast. Table with double pedestal lamp and two oak spindle armchairs with upholstery seats.

Left: Susan Lawrence Dana (Dana-Thomas) House, Springfield, Illinois. Studio looking west. The two special tables were designed for the viewing of Japanese woodblock prints.

Above: Susan Lawrence Dana (Dana-Thomas) House, Springfield, Illinois. Studio music cabinet. The studio was equipped with several bespoke items of furniture such as this cabinet designed to hold sheet music and scores.

Right: Susan Lawrence Dana (Dana-Thomas) House. Main bedroom. The twin beds are screened on each side by portieres and curtains, giving the effect of a four-poster bed

It was, however, in his furniture for work spaces that Wright achieved his most startling designs in his later years, apart, that is, from the furniture that was designed, and part-made in some cases, for the Usonian houses. The two great private houses of his later years, "Wingspread" and Fallingwater were each built for clients for whom he was simultaneously building offices. Both were built to the highest specifications and furnished accordingly. Fallingwater of 1936 was Wright's most important house commission since the Robie House. Built as a summer house for Edgar Kaufmann, the Pittsburgh department store owner, whose son had been an apprentice at Taliesin, Wright was also to design the Kaufmann office inside the family store in Pittsburgh, which in its cave-like, paneled seclusion, forms a markedly different working environment to the transparency of the Kaufmann weekend retreat, Fallingwater. Spectacularly sited and cantilevered over a stream, Wright created a "living space over and above the stream upon

Above: Herbert F. Johnson House ("Wingspread"), Wind Point, Wisconsin. Hearth and built-in seating with hexagonal hassocks. The living spaces are articulated around the central core of the great chimney.

several terraces upon which a man who loved the place sincerely, one who liked to listen to the waterfall, might well live." Particular expertise was needed in the crafting of the built-in furniture, which was of North Carolina walnut and walnut veneer by the Gillen Woodworking Company of Milwaukee. Wright insisted that, in order to prevent moisture damage and prevent warping, the grain of the wood should be

used in horizontal fashion, rather than vertically as was usually the case, and that the usual five-plywood be replaced by nine-ply. In design, the free-standing furniture echoes the cantilevered form of the house and is of exceptionally fine craftsmanship.

The Gillen Woodwork Corporation was also responsible for much of the specially designed free-standing furniture for the spectacular

Above: Herbert F. Johnson House ("Wingspread"). Detail of paneling and built-in seating in the hearth area. There was much emphasis on fine craftsmanship, and the detailing is exceptionally fine.

Herbert F. Johnson House ("Wingspread") near Racine. Here the living area is grouped around a huge central chimney stack with five fire-places, dividing the lofty vertical space into zones to include a family living room, dining room and library, with four wings extending outward from this. The entire plan is oriented so that each of the room spaces would be sunlit for at least part of the day and, as with other houses, the qualities of "Wingspread" are related directly to the nature of the site, which partly determined its form. The site was barely half a mile from Lake Michigan, on a former nature reserve comprising some 30 acres of land that included a ravine and a lake. It would appear that Wright regarded "Wingspread" as a development of the Prairie House of half a century before, although the land it occupies is far more extensive and the form radically transformed, which centered on a reworking of Wright's "sacred hearth" with the monumental brick chimney at its core.

There are also resonances from the Prairie years in some of the furniture that was specially designed for the house. The forms of the building, which use both ovals and hexagonals as modular units, are reflected in the furniture, notably in the tables and hexagonal hassocks of the main living area. Apparently, Wright, on a visit to the Darwin Martin house around 1936, saw the possibilities of adapting the arm-chairs he had designed for a very different setting. The handsome bar-rel chairs, which provide a curved emphasis, echoing the shape of the hearth, were also used in a very similar design at Taliesin.

The chair and desk design for the S.C. Johnson Wax Administration Building are also conceived in terms of the architecture they inhabit. Curves and circles predominate in the design, most notably in the lily-pad like concrete columns of the architecture, and these are reflected in the metal chairs and desks that are still in use throughout the build-ing. The furniture, which is made of cast-aluminum piping soldered together, rather than the tubular steel in use among Wright's peers in furniture design, such as Mies van der Rohe and Marcel Breuer, is also, crucially, painted in the warm russet tone used throughout the building with fabric upholstery in the same color. The chairs and desks are early examples of open-office planning, with some of the multi-layer desk

Above Left: Herbert F. Johnson House ("Wingspread"). Built-in desk area, with barrel chair and floor light. Cypress is the favored wood for both paneling and furniture through-out the house.

Left: Barrel chair from Herbert F. Johnson House ("Wingspread"). Adapted from a design used in an earlier Prairie style house, the chair is part of the dominant design motifs of the house and furniture, which juxtapose ovals and hexagons.

designs indeed anticipating today's work stations. The desk designs reflect the internal and external forms of the building and the integration of furniture and setting, in an inward-looking space flooded with natural light diffused through the tubular glass walls, creates Wright's most harmonious working interior.

Usonian houses were furnished with extraordinary economy, as most of the requisite furnishings were built-in. Some owners, like Herbert and Katherine Jacobs, for whom the first Usonian was built in 1937, near Madison, Wisconsin, had their furniture made by two cousins who had power tools and learned upholstering, "and agreed to do the job for $300." Jacobs kept a complete record of the house and recorded that "Wright saw their plans, and modified the leg and fin design of the dining table, but made no other changes." Free-standing Usonian furniture is often characterized by its "origami" like forms, with shapes that could be put together easily without cabinet-making skills, as in the Prairie houses or indeed the refinements of craft and design of the furniture for his wealthy clients, like Johnson and Kaufmann.

Wright was, however, extraordinarily consistent in his remarkable final years in his creation of harmonious organic designs for living or working, whether it be a typist's desk and chair that would be comfortable and efficient to work at or the finely crafted walnut furniture of Fallingwater.

Left: Herbert F. Johnson House ("Wingspread"), Wind Point, Wisconsin. Built-in seating of the central hearth area with terraces beyond. Wright considered Wingspread to be one of his best-built and costliest houses.

Above left: Jacobs First Residence, Madison, Wisconsin. Living room alcove with built-in shelving and bespoke table and chairs. The modular unit of the house, a two-by-four-foot rectangle, is incised into the concrete floor slab.

Left: Stanley and Mildred Rosenbaum House, Florence, Alabama. Dining area with built-in table and shelves. The built-in cypress table and storage was designed by Wright, while the plywood chairs are by Charles Eames.

CASE STUDY: FRANK LLOYD WRIGHT HOME AND STUDIO

FRANK LLOYD WRIGHT HOME AND STUDIO. HOME
CONSTRUCTED 1889–95. STUDIO CONSTRUCTED
1895–1906.

In 1888, Wright married Catherine Tobin, and with a loan of $5,000 from his architectural mentor, Louis Sullivan, began building a house in the leafy Chicago suburb of Oak Park. The 22-year-old architect was able to put his design principles into practice in what started out originally as a modest, six-room bungalow, which Wright added to and adapted over the next 20 years. A sizeable studio, containing a drafting room, an office for Wright himself, and a library was later added to the house and the complex became both home and working environment for the Wrights and their growing family.

Wright used both house and studio to experiment with ideas and their implementation. However, the working out of his radical experiments with space and form were subject to the practicalities of day-to-day family life. It is clear that the young Wright used the house as a kind of laboratory in which he experimented with ideas, and experienced their reality, before applying the lessons learned to his commissioned work for clients. His most radical designs for both built-in and free standing furniture were first designed for the house and studio, and there are several accounts of his moving the furniture around in both spaces on a regular basis—at least every six months, as the photographs taken at the time attest. The living room, with its focal point of "the sacred hearth," was part of the original structure. As Wright later wrote "really there need be but one room, the living room…openings should occur as integral features of the structure and form, if possible its natural ornamentation." The use of oak throughout provides warmth and visual continuity, as does the use of built-in seating.

By 1895, the Wrights had four children and the domestic space was in obvious need of enlargement. The new dining room is a remarkably intimate space, distinguished by the first of Wright's monumental dining tables surrounded by high-backed chairs of complex design, the antecedents of many such chairs in subsequent years. The dining table was illuminated by another radical design, the first of Wright's many light screens. The dining table, with its set of eight chairs, could be extended for guests. The entire second floor of the new wing was occupied by the barrel-vaulted playroom—15ft (4.5m) high, it is lit by

Above right: Playroom looking west. The lofty barrel-vaulted playroom has extensive ranges of built-in storage for toys and books. The gallery could accommodate a small audience for family entertainments or serve as a musicians' gallery.

Right: Dining room table, chairs, and illuminated ceiling grille. The high-backed chairs, there were eight in the set, are the earliest examples designed by Wright.

an art-glass skylight set in a wooden fretwork ceiling. The windows of the room are set at child height with window seats, while adults must stoop to look out of them. This is an imaginative concept on Wright's part that extends to other features of the room, such as the stair-stepped balcony, scaled for children, and the splendid mural that takes its theme from *The Arabian Nights*. The mural is flanked by glass fronted toy cupboards and the whole room is amply provided with built-in seating and storage.

The studio complex forms a separate entity from the house. Although they are interconnected, each has a separate entrance and a distinctive character of its own.

The burgeoning architectural practice necessitated more working space for Wright and his assistants, as well as a suitably impressive space in which to receive clients and contractors. The complex of rooms indicates the radical development in Wright's thinking, which had accelerated rapidly in a short space of time. The experimental features, such as good natural light and functional desks and chairs were to be the key to the development of the working environments that form such a crucial part of Wright's later work.

Left: Living room seating area. The sense of an uninterrupted flow of space is enhanced by the low ceiling and integrated, built-in upholstered seating.

CASE STUDY: FREDERICK C. ROBIE HOUSE

FREDERICK C. ROBIE HOUSE, CHICAGO, ILLINOIS.
CONSTRUCTED 1908–10.

The Robie House is generally agreed to be the culmination of Wright's conception of the Prairie house. It is remarkable for its many refinements, not least in its adaptation of the extremes of climactic conditions in Chicago. Wright himself stressed the integration of its organic design in his introduction to the influential *Wasmuth Portfolio* of his designs in 1910: "The gently sloping roofs grateful to the Prairie do not leave large air spaces above the rooms, and so the chimney has grown in dimensions and importance and in hot weather ventilates the circulating air-spaces beneath the eaves through openings easily closed in winter." The refinements and practicalities of the brick-built design can be seen in such features as the steeply pitched roof overhang, so designed to provide maximum protection from the powerful Chicago sunlight that even in the middle of summer the midday sun does not

Above right: One of a set of six dining chairs designed for the Frederick C. Robie House, Chicago, Illinois. Severely rectilinear in design, the high backed chairs, with leather upholstered drop-in seats, have nine spindles that run the length of the back beneath a broad crest rail.

Right: Sofa with built-in tables. The marked horizontality of the entire design is emphasized by the wooden banding of the space. The rectilinear motifs of the art-glass windows are repeated as occasional single motifs in the carpet.

Right: Table and two side chairs. Wright designed this small dining area in the "prow" of the living room space, as the Robies regarded the original dining room too grand for everyday use.

52

strike the south-facing dining room. Such control of the elements enables the interior to be lit by an extraordinary series of large windows that are markedly light and elegant in style.

The Robie House perfectly exemplifies Wright's concept that "every house worth considering as a work of art must have a grammar of its own…a great thing instead of a collection of smaller ones." At the Robie House, Wright's commission included designs for the oak furniture, carpeting, and the light fixtures, as well as the window glass throughout the house. Both motifs and color tonalities are drawn from the presiding "grammar" of the dominant geometric designs that prevail throughout the house. Linked motifs appear in the carpet designs and in the window glass. These two-dimensional forms are echoed in the three-dimensional forms of the furniture to produce an extraordinarily integrated whole. Dining and living areas are separated only by the hearth and stairway and the whole space is banded in wood with spherical light fittings illuminating its entire width.

The dining room ensemble, in which the marked horizontal and vertical emphases echo both the original built-in buffet and the external elevations of the house, was altered at some time after the Robies left the house in 1911. Originally, the table had built-in oak piers surmounted by electric lamps, which in the design of their glass echo the art-glass window designs. Such grandeur of design was considered by the Robies to be impractical for everyday use and Wright provided them with a practical built-in dining area or nook in the "prow" of the space.

The supervision and co-ordination of the various elements of the complex, as well as the subtle Robie interiors, was entrusted to the Milwaukee interior decorating firm of Niedecken-Walbridge Co. (who were used by Wright in other Prairie commissions), while the furniture was made by the F.H. Bresler Co., also of Milwaukee; a city well known for its skilled woodcraftsmen, mostly of German origin.

Far left: Seating area and hearth. The space is conceived as a whole with only the hearth providing separation between the seating and dining areas. The horizontality of the continuous oak banding across the space at ceiling level is offset by the motifs in the carpet, which echo the design of the art glass.

Left: Storage, lighting, and art glass in the hearth area, showing the complex integration of motifs and materials of the entire design.

CASE STUDY: POPE LEIGHEY HOUSE

LOREN POPE (POPE LEIGHEY) HOUSE, WOODLAWN
PLANTATION, ALEXANDRIA, VIRGINIA. CONSTRUC-
TED 1940–41.

Like Herbert Jacobs, owner of the first Usonian house to be built, Loren Pope was a journalist. In August 1939 he wrote to Wright with a request for a "Jacobs-style house" and one, moreover, that would be affordable on a salary of $50 a week, "There are certain things a man wants during life, and of life. Material things and things of the spirit…one fervent wish…includes both. It is for a house created by you." The letter brought a ready assent and by November that same year plans for a Usonian house, built on the identical two-by-four-foot rectangular module to that of the Jacobs House, were completed for a site in Falls Church, Virginia. The house of wood, brick, and glass, with the brick fireplace and workspace (which replaced the kitchen area in Usonian houses) at its heart, was built to such a flexible and efficient design that the whole structure was able to be removed and rebuilt on its present site when threatened by the building of an interstate

Above right: Dining area with built-in shelving and extendable table. The dining table stands in front of the French windows to the terrace and is lit from above by recessed downlighters. Modular seating can be moved to form different units.

Right: Work corner with built in desk. Usonian houses were economical in the use of space. Here a corner is utilized and lit by paired plywood lightscreens, placed vertically.

Right: The open-plan living area with flexible seating and views to the garden was a key component of the Usonian house, together with the use of natural materials: brick, wood, concrete, and glass. Distinctive cut-out panels of Cherokee red joinery are used for clerestory windows and light screens.

Right: View of the main living area, looking toward the hearth with the dining area beyond. A distinctive feature of the house is a series of wooden fretwork panels, used here horizontally, to provide a continuous band of clerestory windows at ceiling height.

highway in 1964. Its second owner, Mrs Marjorie Leighey, donated it to the National Trust for Historic Preservation and it was reassembled at its present historic site at Woodlawn Plantation, Mount Vernon in 1965. Although the house is small in size, with a typical Usonian L-shaped plan, there is a spacious living room with paneled ceilings some eleven feet high, and Wright was able to provide "quiet" spaces away from the communal living area.

As with other Usonian designs, most of the furniture was built in. Even the cushioned chairs, which appear to be part of the built-in furniture, were multi-purpose as they could be used as easy chairs in the living area, or placed together as a sofa, or moved to the simple table in the dining area to be used as dining chairs. Twelve chairs were made for the house in 1940, of plywood glued and screwed together and so designed that they could be made on the job site without specialist cabinet-making skills. A distinctive feature of the Pope Leighey House is the use of red cypress board light screens as an integral part of the design. Clerestory windows are formed of horizontal fretwork cutouts that frame views of the surrounding trees. The same abstract cutout motifs are used singly or in vertical pairs to form perforated panels of Cherokee red joinery—a material used throughout the building, which helps create a simple yet highly effective organic whole.

Left: Study area with built-in desk, storage shelves, and drawers. Specially designed modular seating can be moved into flexible arrangements for different activities, while built-in storage was an essential component of the compact Usonian space.

CASE STUDY: THE S.C. JOHNSON WAX ADMINISTRATION BUILDING

THE S.C. JOHNSON WAX ADMINISTRATION BUILDING.
CONSTRUCTED 1936, RACINE.

Both the Administrative Office of 1936–39 and the Research Laboratories tower, which was built between 1944 and 1950, were conceived as streamlined, organic structures. Wright wrote of the entire complex, "Organic architecture designed this great building to be as inspiring a place to work as any cathedral ever was in which to worship," and this analogy is made clear both by the height of the buildings and their use of glass to flood the interior with light. The style and design of the furniture were both an integral part of the design and a radical departure for Wright from his previous designs for what he termed "the sacred place of work." Wright's earliest office building, which provided an inward-looking and perfectly co-ordinated business environment for the Larkin Company in Buffalo, New York, had been built in 1903, and for this he had designed revolutionary new furniture, including some of the earliest metal office furniture.

The Larkin building was described by Wright as a "great fire-proof vault," and the employees of the mail-order company worked at metal desks from metal armchairs with leather seats of angular design. So radical was Wright's approach that he was even to produce a desk with a built-in chair that could be swung back and stored under the desk when not in use. The Johnson Wax headquarters is also an inward-looking light-filled space, but there the comparison with the earlier

Above right: Chair from the S.C. Johnson Administration Building, Racine, Wisconsin. Victoria and Albert Museum, London. The three-legged chair was intended to encourage good posture, by encouraging the sitter to place both feet on the floor. Many of the chairs soon had to have the addition of another leg in the interests of stability, although some of the originals remain in use in the building.

Right: Reception area from a period photograph taken when the building was first opened in 1939. The curves of the hemispherical dome of the ceiling are reflected in the design of the reception desk, table, and chair.

Right: View of the Great Workroom. An early example of an open-plan office, the original desks and chairs are still in use, demonstrating both their utility and their flexibility to the use of new technologies. The Great Workroom is a complete example of Wright's total environment.

60

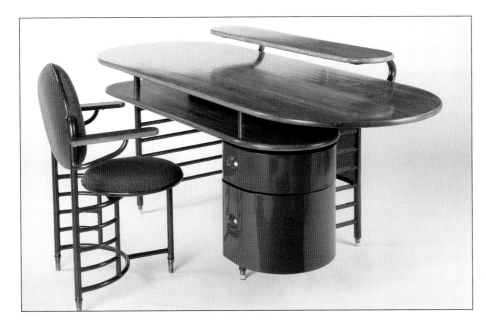

Above: Chair and Desk from the S. C. Johnson Administration Building, Racine, Wisconsin. Victoria and Albert Museum, London. The desk and tubular armchair are designed as a unit and are still in use throughout the building, differing only in the disposition of shelves and ledges. This example has a filing bin that can be swung out from the desk for ease of use.

Right: Reception area, with four chairs in front of glass screen wall. The four-legged armchairs are upholstered in Cherokee red cloth, and as with the chairs throughout the complex, the backs can be pivoted for comfort and to reduce wear on the fabric.

structure (which was demolished in 1950) ends. Three decades earlier the brick-built Larkin building had been essentially of its time in its attitude to the workers it housed in several respects, notwithstanding its great central court, which was lit by skylights throughout its five storeys. The workers in the mail-order company, which produced soap and other household products, were exhorted by carved homiletic texts such as: "INTELLIGENCE ENTHUSIASM CONTROL" and "COOPERATION ECONOMY INDUSTRY."

The Johnson Wax workers are housed in naturally lit spaces with furniture that harmonizes perfectly with the curved, streamlined shapes of the architecture.

The circular motifs are carried through the design of all the furniture with extraordinary consistency, from the pivoting backs of the chairs to the tubular steel of the chair supports and the curved desk drawers, which can be swung forward to the curved maple tops of the desks on parallel levels. The tubular and wooden elements of the furniture, in their turn, echo the radical Pyrex tubing that illuminates the building.

The design of the three-legged chair, with and without arms, is particularly remarkable. The chair was originally designed to encourage good posture, with the sitter's legs firmly on the floor. If the unfortunate sitter changed position, the most likely result was that the chair was capsized. Although the original design made an especially aesthetically pleasing ensemble with the desk, many of the chairs have since had the addition of an extra leg in the interests of stability. The practicality of the furniture design throughout the building is attested by the fact that it is still in use.

CASE STUDY: FALLINGWATER AND THE KAUFMANN OFFICE

FALLINGWATER, OHIOPYLE. CONSTRUCTED 1935.
THE KAUFMANN OFFICE, PITTSBURGH.
CONSTRUCTED 1937.

Fallingwater (1936) was Wright's most important domestic commission since the Robie House. In 1938 Wright described in *The Architectural Forum* that he had "created a living space over and above the stream upon several terraces upon which a man who loved the place sincerely, one who like to listen to the waterfall, might well live." The client, Edgar Kaufmann, was a Pittsburgh store owner whose son had been a fellow at Taliesin. Edgar Kaufmann Jr. initiated several family commissions and his long working relationship with Wright was continued through publications after his death in 1989. Kaufmann Jr. was responsible for his parents' initial interest in Wright's work and it was soon recognized that his father needed a working environment as well as the spectacular summer and weekend retreat provided by Fallingwater. Originally, Fallingwater and the office were designed as parallel projects in 1935. However, the apparently straightforward office project was subject to several delays and was not completed for another two years. It was another six months before all the specially designed furniture was moved into the space, which was built into the northwest corner of the store on the tenth floor.

While Fallingwater is justly famous as an American icon, other projects for Kaufmann were unrealized. The Kaufmann Office, which was reconstructed in the Victoria and Albert Museum after being

Right: Office of Edgar J. Kaufmann, from Kaufmann's Department Store, Pittsburgh, Pennsylvania. Victoria and Albert Museum, London. Wright's design principles are shown in the integrated decoration of the room and the use of materials, which include veneered plywood, rayon, and cotton chenille upholstery in a natural state, as well as the use of machine-made standardized parts.

Right: Office of Edgar J. Kaufmann. The woodwork of the office, including the mural, which acts as the focus of the windowless space, the built-in desk, and the huge chairs are made from hollow-core plywood veneered with swamp cypress.

Above: Fallingwater. Living room. The use of materials in a refined yet honest state is seen in such details as the floor, which is covered in flagstones of a similar color and texture to the stones in the bed of the stream.

donated by Edgar J. Kaufman Jr. in 1973, is the first entire twentieth-century room to enter the world-renowned collection, and the first Wright interior to be placed on public view in Europe.

As a weekend retreat, Fallingwater had to be both spectacular and easy to maintain. Wright made use of one of his favorite forms of furnishing, the built-in, in spaces throughout the house, from the guest rooms to the 48-foot-long living room. These included shelves and seating, all made of walnut, a material used also in the finely crafted tables and footstools. Built-ins also feature in the design for Mr Kaufmann's office, notably in its key design feature, Kaufmann's monumental desk together with the spectacular wood mural, while the entire organic design reflects the taste and status of owner.

Unlike other Wright work environments, such as the Johnson Wax Office for Herbert Johnson, which was designed between 1936 and 1939, the Kaufmann office does not relate to the rest of the building —indeed its floors, walls, and ceilings had to be specially made to form a sanctuary for the owner, which was removed from the bustle of the store.

The forms of the furniture ultimately derive from Wright's designs of the Prairie period in their monumental and severely rectilinear form. This is particularly noticeable in the overall design of the chairs, although the detailing of the cypress grained wood of both chairs and stools is reminiscent of Wright's contemporary designs for cut-out plywood furniture. Mr Kaufmann's desk, some 10 feet wide in its unextended form is the dominant feature of the room and connects to the mural wall.

By the time the office was completed, in 1938, Wright's reputation had blossomed: Fallingwater was the subject of an exhibition at the Museum of Modern Art and Wright himself appeared on the cover of *Time*. When Kaufmann Jr. had first interested his father in Wright's work, times were hard and he had no buildings under construction, however the Kaufmans continued to support Wright until his death with both cash donations and domestic and civic commissions. Kaufmann Sr. had long cherished a plan to improve civic amenities, in Pittsburgh, for example, but Fallingwater and the Kaufmann Office were all that was completed.

Above: The living room is particularly spacious, some 48 feet in length. The built-in shelves, tables and stools are exceptionally finely crafted from walnut, a material used throughout the building.

GLASS

UNITY TEMPLE, SUSAN LAWRENCE DANA (DANA-THOMAS) HOUSE, ENNIS BROWN HOUSE, SIDNEY BAZETT HOUSE, S.C. JOHNSON WAX ADMINISTRATION BUILDING.

2

Glass is the material which, above all

others, defines the style and design of the work of Frank Lloyd Wright; from the spectacular art glass in his earliest houses in the first decade of the twentieth century to the dome of his last great commission, the Solomon R. Guggenheim Museum, some 60 years later.

Wright used advances in glass technology in the achievement of one of his prime objectives, that of the breaking down of the conventional "box" of room spaces, in both public and private buildings. Wright wanted to open up the flow of spaces between internal areas and dissolve the boundaries between the building and its surroundings where this was appropriate. Fallingwater brilliantly demonstrates the duality of "vista without, vista within" that is so marked a feature of his work. In houses on suburban sites or in public buildings, where it was sometimes crucial to create an inward-looking space, Wright used glass to achieve a flow of natural light from top-lit spaces, while opening up private façades with the aid of a continuous screen of windows.

Wright's earliest use of glass in domestic buildings was naturalistic in the stylized forms it employed, often using leaf and plant forms with

Above right: Aline Barnsdall "Hollyhock House," Los Angeles, California. Detail of play-porch windows seen against the light, showing details of the caming.

Right: Aline Barnsdall "Hollyhock House". Detail of play-porch door, showing the distinctive hollyhock color palette and abstracted flower forms used in the design elements throughout the house

Right: Don and Virginia Lovness House, Stillwater, Minnesota. Interior view of the main living area, showing the floor-to-ceiling windows, the clerestory windows at ceiling level, and the subtle use of top lighting. The house is one of several Usonians to which the owners contributed do-it-yourself skills.

occasional contrasting textures of frosted and clear glass. These early patterns were derived from the work of Wright's master, Louis Sullivan, with whom he trained from 1888 to 1893, and who imbued in him a philosophy of design that remained with Wright throughout his life. In the year Wright left Sullivan's office, Chicago was in the midst of an unprecedented building boom, hosting the World's Columbian Exposition, or Chicago's World's Fair, which brought twenty-seven million visitors to the "White City." Wright was part of a radical circle at the forefront of the city's development and shared many of his clients' concerns about raising young families in modern, well-designed homes that would reflect current thinking on such matters as health, leisure, and the ethical dimensions of the domestic domain.

Wright's clients included such self-made men as the inventor William Wilmslow, who devised a process of electro-glazing that was to become part and parcel of Wright's early art-glass designs, which were innovative, brilliant, and widely copied. Wright explained the theory and practice of his designs in 1908, (*In the Cause of Architecture*): "The windows usually are provided with characteristic straight line patterns, absolutely in the flat and usually severe. The nature of the glass is taken into account in these designs as is also the metal bar used in their construction, and most of them are treated as metal 'grilles' with glass inserted forming a simple rhythmic arrangement of straight lines and squares made as cunning as possible so long as the result is quiet."

Electroglazing achieved such "quiet" results by utilizing straight zinc cames to hold the glass rather than the customary lead cames that were broader, thicker, and more curvilinear. The staining of the glass too was "quiet." Wright preferred sharp, clear colors to enhance his abstracted forms, rather than the darker, more naturalistic palette favored by such contemporaries as Tiffany. The overall effect of the glass in these early designs is a vital contributory factor in Wright's achievement of his style and design principles of "simplicity and repose" in buildings both public and private.

The designs that emanated from Wright's studio in Oak Park until he left Illinois in 1909 were to transform domestic design and create new models for living both in the United States and (with the develop-

Above: Lowell and Agnes Walter House ("Cedar Rock"), Quasqueton, Iowa. The garden room, the major living room of the house. The pierced skylights of the concrete roof and the continuous run of clerestory windows help flood the space with light from above.

Left: Lowell and Agnes Walter House ("Cedar Rock"). Exterior view of garden room showing the screen of floor-to-ceiling plate glass windows opening on to the terrace on the river side of the house.

ment of these new designs for what were to be termed "Prairie Houses") to a worldwide market far beyond the suburbs of Chicago. Much of the success of these early designs lay in their "exotic" use of space and light, the "breaking the box," and to their sympathetic use of natural materials, which was in such strict contrast to the constraints of the general run of domestic architecture of the time. Especially remarkable was Wright's treatment of the windows, or fenestration, of the building. He particularly detested traditionally double-hung windows, terming these "guillotine windows" and deeming that the way in which the light fell through such windows could only be seen as coming through a hole in the wall rather than as a band of light—an extension of the room space and its relation to the exterior world.

Above and left: George Barton House, Buffalo, New York. Detail of living room window design. The variety of iridescent and art glass used exploits different qualities of light, seen (left) from the exterior and (above) against the light.

Wright was to characterize his early clients as men of "unspoiled instincts and untainted ideals," men such as William Winslow, of the Luxfer prism, who was, like Wright himself, a self-made man and for whom he built his first independent project, the William H. Winslow House. The Winslow House, in River Forest, Illinois, allowed Wright unprecedented freedom at the age of 26 to design a house that can be seen to mark a watershed in Wright's career. This can be seen in the flow of its interior spaces achieved by its use of classical motifs and the remarkable use of glass, which is especially striking in the conservatory. Here the curved bay gives way to the "vista without" through a series of identical casement windows between columns. Each frames the view in an identical pattern of elegant abstract plant forms, proving, if proof were needed, the superiority of Wright's favored casements.

Casement windows were used throughout the Home and Studio complex of Wright's Oak Park years. Here the finest and most innovative art glass is used in the studio, which acted as a showcase for Wright's work. Wright's own studio contains his most spectacular and advanced glass in the whole home and studio complex. The triptych of windows, which Wright faced as he worked, is formed of bright green and amber glass in a design constructed of squares, rectangles, and bars. The view from the central window is framed in a manner that perfectly exemplifies Wright's dictum that "a window pattern should stay severely put" and "not get mixed up with the view outside."

Wright's glass designs were executed with the assistance of some remarkable craftsmen. Wright's most lasting partnership was with the Italian designer, Orlando Giannini (of the glass stainers, Giannini and

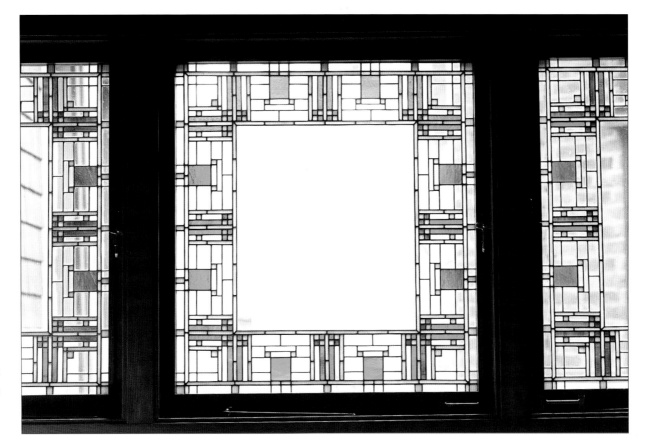

Right: Frank Lloyd Wright Home and Studio, Oak Park, Illinois. Studio window triptych. Wright's own studio contains the most spectacular and radical glass designs of the whole complex. The three casement windows form the focal point of the room, focusing the view through the clear plate glass.

Above: Frank Lloyd Wright Home and Studio, Oak Park, Illinois. Drafting room interior. The skylights and top-lighting of the space diffuse natural light to provide a perfect working light for an architectural practice.

Left: Frank Lloyd Wright Home and Studio. Studio skylights. The rectilinear patterns of gold, sage, and amber glass of the studio reception room diffuse the light through tapestry-like forms that are interspersed with clear glass.

Hilgart) and is seen at its most extraordinary in the designs for the Prairie houses. The complex entrance vestibule of the Frank Thomas House of 1901 at Oak Park is a prime example of Giannini and Hilgart's skills. Wright's conception of glass used as a continuous shimmering screen is realized in spectacular fashion. In what amounts to an almost unbroken band of glass—Wright's idea of an apparently continuous flow of space in which the walls seem to disappear is achieved in the form of a light-diffusing screen. Giannini and Hilgart's specialist skills are evident in the use of opalescent glass, gold-leaf, and mother of pearl

applied in varying degree to the stylized geometric forms. Wright's other collaborative art-glass partnership, that with the Linden Glass Company, produced the most complex and extravagant glass ensembles of the Oak Park years, those for the Susan Lawrence Dana House.

Wright's final Prairie houses in the Chicago area, before he ruptured his strong links with Chicago in 1909, include such extraordinary designs as the Robie House, the May House, and perhaps most interesting of all in terms of the manner in which glass is used, the windows for the Coonley Playhouse of 1912, one of his most famous and engaging designs. Working with the Linden Glass Company, Wright produced what he was to term his "Kindersymphony" for Mrs Ferry Coonley's cottage school, which was run on progressive lines and, sadly, was only used for a few years. The windows were in the main sold to museums, where it is difficult to appreciate the original effect of the dozens of windows that formed the brilliant ensemble. Wright's sojourn in Europe, from 1909 to 1910, undoubtedly had an effect on the design, which is unlike any seen before in his work, although variations on the curvilinear forms were to remain both in architecture and decorative design for the rest of his life. The uncharacteristic use of primary color and fragmented abstract forms draw on a quintessential American phenomenon—the parade. The balloons and confetti motifs are exciting and celebratory in a form particularly appropriate to the medium and to the windows' purpose in a child-centered space.

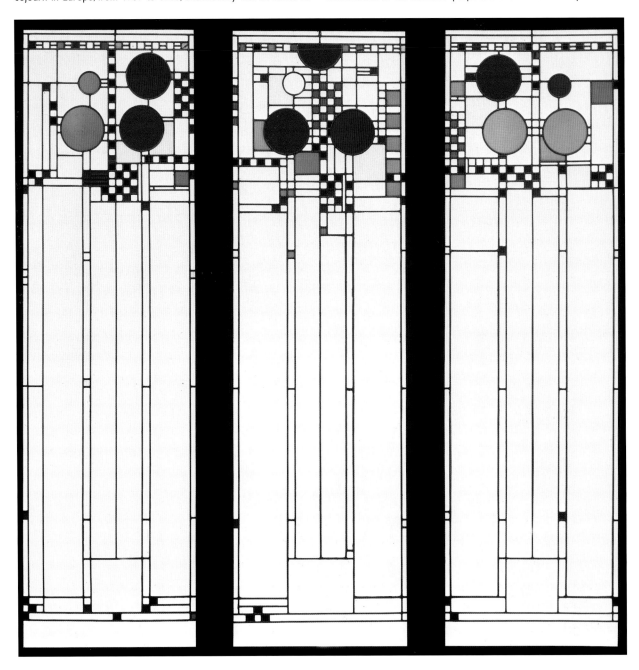

Right: Avery Coonley Playhouse, Riverside, Illinois. The spherical shapes and primary colors of this celebrated design, as well as the motifs of balloons and confetti, represented a radical departure in Wright's work.

The Coonley Playhouse windows also represented a tour de force of glass making for the Linden Glass studios. The spherical shapes in particular presented problems endemic to the materials used. The glass includes flash opal glass and is held in flat zinc cames. The windows represent a pivotal point in the use of glass in Wright's career, one in which he turned away from the abstraction of plant forms, as developed in his work of the Prairie years, and toward an ever increasing abstraction and an emphasis on pure, irreducible forms.

These characteristics are developed in the last great phase of Wright's work with art glass, the California textile block houses, categorized by Wright as "California Romanza," a term that refers to Wright's distinctively romantic interpretation of the dramatic sites and their cultural antecedents, as well as the requirements of his clients. Only two of the houses use art glass, each to spectacular effect and for the final design, that for the Mabel and Charles Ennis House (the Ennis Brown House) Wright almost certainly employed the talents of his trusted glass-maker of the Oak Park years, Orlando Giannini, who is known to have been living in La Jolla at the same time as Wright during the period in which the house was constructed. Certainly the splendid glass mosaic overmantel in the colonnade would appear to be from Giannini's workshop and the main dining room window, which commands a spectacular view of Los Angeles is framed in a triptych form, familiar from Wright's work with Giannini from the Oak Park years.

The other textile block houses do not employ art glass. However, Wright uses clear glass in novel and exciting ways to develop his design ethos in an unexpected manner that was to link with later designs. The small house built for Samuel and Harriet Freeman, the last of the textile block houses, is a compact house, built on a steep site, so designed that it, and its terraces, are perfectly integrated into the hillside. The interior of the house is designed in true Wright fashion to provide both the idea of shelter and the vista within, so central to Wright's domestic dwellings, and to maximize the "vista without" as it is so oriented that the main living room windows command spectacular views of Los Angeles. The glazed and perforated blocks that form the structure of the house are set in counterpoint to the extensive areas of glazing. The

Left: Samuel Freeman House, Hollywood, California. View of the living room. The space is lit by both perforated and glazed blocks in the dominant flower motif of the house, flanking a large picture window to the terrace. Clerestory windows in the same patterned block provide more daylight at ceiling level.

mullions of these windows exactly mirror the lines of the concrete blocks, forming a new and exciting variant on a quintessential Wrightian design element, that of the glass screen. The corners of the building are particularly distinctive as the glass appears to continue around the building, thus literally "breaking the box," and contributing to the lightness of the design and belying the weight and density of the concrete. The living room is lit by both perforated blocks on the main level and by clerestory windows above. Both have the same pattern, forming light and shadow designs of extraordinary variety at different times of day.

Wright carried over the lessons learned in the Freeman House to the Usonian houses of the Depression and post-war years, using very different construction materials, while the creative use of glass to "break the box" is developed in spectacular fashion at Fallingwater, where glass is a crucial element in the design.

In *The Natural House*, Wright declared that "the best way to light a house is God's way—the natural way, as nearly as possible in the daytime and at night as nearly like the day as may be, or better." Such a "natural way" would seem to define the use of perforated panels and screens in the moderately priced designs for the Usonian houses, where all ornament was integral to the structure and had to be economical to produce without employing costly skilled labor in the process. As one of the fundamental principles of the Usonian house was affordability, many owners were encouraged to participate in the building of their homes. Space and money were at a premium in most of the Usonian designs: while each house was of a generic type, such integral details as the fenestration design were unique to each house, as were the perforated motifs that form the defining ornament. A distinctive feature of the very first Usonian house, the Jacobs House built in 1936 for the modest cost of £5,500 were the windows, which, in common with the later Usonian houses (which were built in 17 states) presented an open and closed façade that differentiated the private and public aspects of the building. The façade on the private side of the typical Usonian house uses extensive ranges of floor-to-ceiling windows, while the public façade uses clerestory windows and a modest entrance to ensure privacy.

The style and design of the Usonian house demonstrates Wright's radical rethinking of the place of the family house in changing times, and nowhere is this more apparent than in the use of glass. The Prairie houses, for example had presented an affluent public façade and a clearly defined entrance to the street, often with sparkling displays of art-glass windows, while the Californian textile block houses of the 1920s, which were often built on seemingly inaccessible sites, presented a fortress-like appearance. The typical Usonian house appeared closed on the public façade while remaining true to a central tenet of Wright's philosophy, that of "shelter in the open," propounded by Wright in 1931 in response to changed times. He declared that the modern family house had no need to "box up or hole in," as "security in every sense" was to be found in "free wide spacing and integral construction… Spaciousness is for safety as well as for beauty."

While Wright was working on cost-saving solutions for the average American home that were notably modest in scale and aspiration, he received a unique commission from the father of one of his first Taliesin apprentices, Edgar J. Kaufmann Jr., that was to give new life to Wright's career. The Kaufmann parents visited the Wrights at Taliesin, where, in their son's words "they were moved by the extraordinary beauty of Wright's home and its landscape, and impressed by the devoted enthusiasm of his apprentices." Several projects were discussed, "one was a country house to replace a rudimentary cottage that had served for over a decade." Wright visited the site at Bear Run, Pennsylvania, in December 1934 and wrote to Kaufmann: "The visit to the waterfall in the woods stays with me, and a domicile has taken vague shape in my mind to the music of the stream. When contours come you will see it." The stream and the water cascading into it immediately beneath the house are crucial elements in the design of Fallingwater, which was to become an icon of American architecture. It is the ultimate organic building, at one with its landscape setting, which unusually, Wright left entirely alone.

Glass is a key element in the design of Fallingwater, where transparency was all-important. As the structure of the house rests on a supportive core, rather than load-bearing walls, the exterior walls could be virtually made of glass as long as they were sealed and weath-erproof, thus proving the acme of Wright's philosophy of "shelter in the open," that a house should provide cave-like shelter and yet be open to nature. Fallingwater provides an extraordinarily dynamic connection between an uncompromisingly Modern building and a wild landscape. As Wright himself wrote, "once organic character is achieved in the world of art, that work is for ever. Like sun, moon and stars, great trees, flowers, grass is, and stays on while and wherever man is." Alas, as with several other Wright buildings, the daring construction of Fallingwater has proved less than eternal and it is currently the subject of a rescue-operation that is expected to cost $11.5 million.

Another daring design, which uses glass as an essential part of its structure, is the Headquarters building for Johnson's Wax between 1936 and 1939 and the linked commission for "Wingspread," the house Wright built for Herbert F. Johnson, grandson of the founder of Johnson's Wax, and its president. As with the contemporary commissions of Fallingwater and the office Wright designed for Edgar J. Kaufmann Jr., the patronage of both Johnson and Kaufmann was both pivotal and remarkably productive at this stage in Wright's career, resulting in some of his finest and most celebrated work and bringing him back into the forefront of public opinion. "Wingspread" was the most expensive and largest domestic commission to date, built in 1937, of brick and steel in a series of planar forms around a central brick core, with much emphasis on craftsmanship and a unique employment of glass throughout its structure.

The planar forms of the Prairie house may still be recognized in "Wingspread." However, in the headquarters building for the S.C. Johnson Company of 1936–9, and the Research Tower of 1944, Wright used a circular module throughout, from the top-lighting that filters through the famous lily-pad columns of the Great Workroom to the unique furniture that Wright designed for the building. However, it is the use of circular forms for the glass that renders the building so inno-vative and justly famous. The young Wright had been fascinated by the possibilities offered by the Luxfer prism, before electricity was widely available for the lighting of public buildings. Forty-two years later,

Right: Herbert F. Johnson House, Wind Point, Wisconsin. View of central octagon and clerestory windows from the hearth area. There was a unique employment of glass throughout the structure, which otherwise used brick, cypress, and pink Kasota sandstone as its building materials.

Wright seized the opportunity of using the new technology of Pyrex glass tubing to filter the light instead of flat glass prisms, a brilliant device which serves to further "break the box" of the structure.

As with the early Larkin Administration Building of 1904, and Unity Temple of five years later, the Johnson Administration building had to be inward-looking by reason of its busy and noisy site. Wright himself insisted that there were to be no windows in the building, instead natural light is filtered through Pyrex tubes. This is particularly striking in the Great Workroom, which is lit from the wide bands of Pyrex tubing that light the central space and, most radically, in the top-lighting of the roof, where similar tubes fill the space between the extraordinary lily-pad concrete columns and the ceiling. The Pyrex tubes provided not only light but insulation in the semicircular roof of glass tubes that form the pedestrian bridge, linking the publicity department and the executive penthouse. Both here and in the spectacular hemispherical domed ceiling of the reception area of the publicity department, Lumiline tubes were inserted between two layers of glass tubing to illuminate the building at night by diffusing electric light, simulating the effect of sunlight.

In his last years, Wright was commissioned to design several major public buildings in which the use of glass was to play a crucial part. In the Beth Sholom Synagogue (Elkins Park, Pennsylvania, completed in 1959), for example, he conceived the structure as a huge translucent pyramid-like form, completely free of internal support and roofed in glass with a striking central "wings" feature of brilliantly illuminated stained glass in resonant symbolic colors. The triangular form of this design repeats the basic triangular module that informs the entire building, from the ground plan itself to the integrated ornament. The very last building Wright designed in 1957, and by far the largest of his career, the Marin County Civic Center, San Rafael, California, demonstrates that Wright's innovatory response to challenge remained radical to the very end. The monumental complex, which houses the

Right: Beth Sholom Synagogue, Elkins Park, Pennsylvania. Wright himself referred to the structure of the huge building as "a lighted mountain." The vast, pyramidal form, which is entirely free of internal support, is roofed in glass that filters the light through translucent panels.

county offices, the courts of justice, the central library, a jail, and other civic spaces, is contained in two huge wings linked by a light-filled central court. The spectacular site spans three hills and accommodates fairgrounds and a man-made lagoon that flows from the fountain sited on the cafeteria terraces. The building offers both a congenial working environment and an appropriate interface for the public. Much of its ambience is provided by the use of glass, while top-lighting, via huge continuous skylights and a series of light wells, penetrates through three floors throughout the complex.

Light wells had been a constant feature of Wright's designs for what he termed "the sacred place of work." In the Johnson Wax Administrative Building the use of glass had diffused natural light within an environment that eliminated views of the outside in order to concentrate the workforce on the task in hand. Twenty years later Wright provided every office, however humble, with a view, whether to the hills and valleys of the "vista without" or of the enclosed light-filled mall that forms the "vista within." The promenades that run between the buildings are also illuminated from a translucent skylight, or more precisely roof light, that floods the space with light sufficient for the growth of an extensive formal planting at ground-floor level. Extensive views of the surrounding countryside are provided at third-floor level through cut-out windows in the eaves of the roof.

1959, the year of Wright's death at the age of 92, finally saw the opening of the most significant and controversial of the buildings of his last decade, The Solomon Guggenheim Museum in New York. The building had taken 16 years of struggle to realize Wright's dream of "the substance of an atmosphere for a form" and the original design went through many trials and tribulations. A particular loss was the design for the original dome of the 1945 project, which was formed of concentric circles of tubular glass, part of Wright's concept of the natural light diffused from the dome to the central space giving the illusion of a "fluid environment." This is reminiscent of the lighting of the Great Workroom of the Johnson Wax Administration building, which has been said to evoke the ambience of an underwater environment beneath the great lily-pad capitals of the lofty columns.

Wright believed that works of art were best experienced in the changing conditions of natural light, a truth to which most of the great galleries of the world attest. The top-lighting of traditional gallery spaces can today be enhanced by computer-controlled lighting that responds to changes in the light as they occur. Wright's solution to the problem of lighting the museum was intended to replicate natural light as far as possible, and to that end the radical glass tube technology used in the Johnson Wax building was developed in the design for the skylights or "rifts," which ran the entire length of the ramp on its outer edge. Enclosing a system of incandescent glass tubes, they subtly enhance the natural light that floods through the space from the monumental hemispherical dome, the key to the whole "skyward" expansion of the great central space.

The interior of the Guggenheim creates its own tranquil world in opposition to its site, recalling the concrete-built and glass-roofed Unity Temple of 50 years before. Here, too, Wright turned the building inward, shutting out the external environment entirely. Wright elaborated on the paradox thus, "the impression made upon one" (by the interior space and light of the building) "is similar to that made by a still wave, never breaking, never offering resistance or finality to vision." It is that extraordinary quality of the complete repose known only in movement that characterizes this building. The "unbroken wave" of the spiral ramp begins and ends in the lens-shaped pool and fountain at its base, a focal point that is rhymed with the translucent space of the monumental central dome, all designed to create a total environment and, in Wright's words, "a new unity between beholder, painting and architecture."

CASE STUDY: UNITY TEMPLE

UNITY TEMPLE, OAK PARK, ILLINOIS.
CONSTRUCTED 1905.

The idea of windows being used to produce a band of continuous light may be seen in Unity Temple, the major public building of Wright's years at Oak Park. Unity Temple was a significant commission for Wright's small studio in 1905 and one that was particularly exacting in its use of glass. The Unitarian-Universalist congregation had only a modest budget of some $45,000 and this necessitated the use of economic building materials. The solid masonry of reinforced concrete decided upon was turned to brilliant effect both in the aesthetics of the design and the practical need for a peaceful space, on what was then a heavily trafficked site.

Wright himself saw Unity Temple as a watershed in his career. Interviewed some 50 years after it was built, he reflected: "I think that was about the first time when the interior space began to come through as the reality of that building. When you sat in Unity Temple you were sitting under a big concrete slab but your eyes go out into the clouds on four sides. There were no walls with holes in them." Today, almost 100 years later, the visitor is immediately made aware, on entering the building, of the continuity between the outside world and the inner sanctum of the temple by the use of Wright's characteristic "light screens," which here take the form of art-glass windows and doors.

Wright conceived the Temple as a cube, "a noble form of masonry." The overhead structure is carried on four hollow concrete posts, enabling the walls to be non-supporting and to act as screens, an effect further enhanced by the band of light screens immediately below the roof, which form a clerestory or "clearstory," as in a medieval cathedral. Wright's use of art glass in the top-lighting and in the side alcoves was intended, as he himself wrote, "to get a sense of a happy cloudless day into the room…daylight sifting through between the intersecting concrete beams, filtering through amber glass ceiling lights. Thus managed, the light would, rain or shine, have the warmth of sunlight."

The simple, yet powerful geometry of the spatial design is further integrated by the use of solid spheres, squares, and cubes in the glass light fittings, while the golden and amber tones of the whole extend to

the minute and painstaking detail of the gold silk that covers the wiring of the lamp fixtures. Wright called Unity Temple his "jewel box," a description that extends from the smallest detail to the magnificent coffered skylights, which form the entire ceiling. Of amber and beige glass, the pattern of squares and rectangles echoes the Froebel Gifts that inspired the powerful geometry of the whole design. Each is subtly set at a different angle to the whole.

Above right: The continuous band of art-glass windows beneath the amber glass ceiling skylights was intended, as Wright put it, "to get a sense of a happy cloudless day into the room…Thus managed the light would, rain or shine, have the warmth of sunlight."

Right: Roof skylights. The pierced and coffered ceiling is formed of skylights of amber and beige glass in a pattern of squares and rectangles, each is set at a different angle to the whole.

CASE STUDY: SUSAN LAWRENCE DANA (DANA-THOMAS) HOUSE

Wright was given almost free rein and an unlimited budget by the wealthy socialite Susan Lawrence Dana for a house in which to entertain her prestigious social and political circle on a lavish scale. The generous budget allowed Wright to employ the Linden Glass Company's expertise, with some 450 bespoke art-glass panels and some 200 custom-made light fittings for the house. The grand residence, which took two years to complete in its entirety, comprised 35 rooms of wonderful variety and intricacy. Throughout the house, the use of glass in the major social spaces is instrumental in creating a flow of light and opening up the interior. This begins with the entrance itself, where the function of the house, as a suitable setting for a society and political hostess, and an important social focus for the area, may be read into the interlocking butterfly forms of the glass of the entrance arch, which may have been intended to represent Susan Lawrence Dana's status as a social butterfly. Wright exploits the decorative possibilities of iridescent glass in the splendid fanlight, which appears green and blue in tone from outside and amber and pale gold against the light of the exterior.

Right: Entrance transom seen against the light. The butterfly motifs used in the design are used throughout the house, together with flower motifs to bring natural forms inside the house and to compensate for the lack of natural vegetation on the site.

Right: Detail of butterfly motifs, which form the design of the art-glass arch of the entrance corridor, seen against the light.

Inside, the great barrel-vaulted space of the dining room is lit by clerestory windows, where Wright employs the prairie flower, the sumac, together with the fall tones used throughout the house, in a series of repeating motifs. The arched window below the vault also carries sumac designs that offer subtle variations of color on the prevailing motifs in the same distinctive coloration.

However splendid the glass elsewhere in the house, it was the art glass of the fountain doors and windows that the Linden Gall Company chose to exemplify their work in the advertisements for the company. The ensemble comprises four windows and six doors, and here the motif is not that of the upright prairie sumac but pendant flowers resembling wisteria, or possibly, from their coloration, laburnum.

The windows of the studio form a marked contrast to the glass elsewhere in the house. The series of panels appear to be suspended from the caming of the upper registers of the window for which Wright coined the term "suspended glass screen" while the design employs plant-like abstractions unique in Wright's work. The art glass of the Dana House is the most opulent as well as the most complete example of Wright's work during the Prairie Style years.

Above: Detail of fountain doors. Instead of the upright forms of the sumac plant, used throughout the rest of the house, the fountain room employs a distinctive pendant flower motif which recalls wisteria, or from its coloration, laburnum.

Right: Studio windows. This series of nine panels, which uses plant-like abstractions, was described by Wright as a "suspended glass screen," as it appears to hang, suspended from hook-like forms against the light. The design is unique in Wright's work.

Right: Detail of dining room windows. The double motifs are formed of abstractions of the prairie sumac plan, which is used throughout the design of the house in many of its constituent elements as a unifying motif.

Right: Dining room windows. The repeated design of the bay windows is that of the prairie sumac plant, the unifying motif of the entire house. The double motifs are formed of abstractions of the leaves, stems, and flowers of the plant, all in distinctive fall colorations. The space was used as a breakfast room by Mrs Dana.

CASE STUDY: ENNIS BROWN HOUSE

MABEL AND CHARLES ENNIS HOUSE (ENNIS BROWN
HOUSE). CONSTRUCTED 1923–24.

The Ennis Brown residence was the last house designed by Wright to incorporate art glass. Designed in 1923, it is the grandest and most monumental of all the textile block houses and the last of the genre. Conspicuous on its ridge in the Santa Monica Mountains, the house is in fact smaller in scale than it appears. Wright had always sought dramatic sites, which heightened, in his words, "the true property of character." The drama inherent in the site is reflected in the architecture, for which Wright used a form of stacked textile patterned blocks with forms reminiscent of Mayan motifs, although the design is one of the most eclectic and fantastic of all Wright's works. As one of the futuristic settings for Ridley Scott's *Blade Runner* of 1982, it achieved iconic status in the collective memory almost six decades after it was built.

Wright's final use of art glass is as spectacular as the building and the site it commands, moreover there are links with his earliest commissions in Illinois. He may well have employed the talents of his trusted glass maker of the Oak Park years, Orlando Giannini, who is known to have been living in La Jolla at the same time the building was constructed. The abstract motifs in the glass—notably that of the living room, in the smaller dining room windows, and in the library doors and windows—may be seen as partially derived from plant forms indigenous to the area, as with the early art-glass designs for such houses as the Susan Lawrence Dana residence.

Above right: Detail of art glass seen against the light, showing the contrast of the clear glass panes with the delicate caming and tiny points of scintillating color.

Right: Dining room window seen from the exterior. The towering glass window commands a superb view of Los Angeles through clear glass panes, with scintillating points of art glass in a palette unique in Wright's work to provide interest in the diagonal forms of the caming.

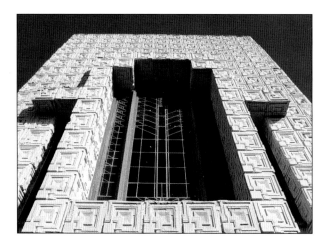

Right: Detail of side panels of the window triptych of the main dining room. The diagonal forms of the design of the art glass in the upper and lower register of the window are pure abstractions and are set against panes of clear glass.

Right: Living room glass, showing the abstract motifs derived from plant forms and distinctive blue-green colorations that are unique in Wright's designs for art glass.

The main dining room window frames a spectacular view of Los Angeles in a triptych form, familiar from Wright's early work, such as that in his own studio at Oak Park. The diagonal forms incorporated into the design are reminiscent of those used in the "Hollyhock" House, but these are pure abstractions, with a symmetry, harmony, and balance that might be termed classical. The caming is delicate with subtle variations of width and the scintillating points of color of the tiny glass fragments are set in satisfying counterpoint against the clear panes. The attention to style and design detail in the art glass throughout the house may be seen not only to the big set piece ensembles, such as that of the dining room, but in that given to more mundane areas. The bathroom windows, for example, frame geometric forms in the coloration used throughout the art glass in the house with textured panes to form a privacy screen.

Left: Detail of window glass showing abstract forms derived from plants in a manner reminiscent of Prairie house designs. The subtleties of color are also reminiscent of the earlier glass and this may point to the collaboration of Wright's trusted glass maker of the Oak Park years, Orlando Giannini.

Above: Detail of bathroom windows. The attention to detail throughout the house is exemplified by the windows of the bathroom in which the scintillating points of color in the palette seen throughout the house are here set against textured glass panes to form a privacy screen.

Right: Detail of art glass. The delicate diagonal tracery of the caming and the distinctive color palette are unique in Wright's work.

Left: Dining room window with view of Los Angeles beyond. The floor-to-ceiling central window is framed in a classically balanced manner by two symmetrical panels.

CASE STUDY: SIDNEY BAZETT HOUSE

SIDNEY BAZETT (BAZETT-FRANK) HOUSE,
HILLSBOROUGH, CALIFORNIA, CONSTRUCTED 1939.

Like its predecessor, the Hanna House, Wright's second house in the San Francisco area was built on a hexagonal module. It is a compact variant on the "diagonal plan" Usonian, the inline "T" or "L" shaped plan, which had originally been built on a rectangular module as in the first Usonian, the Jacobs House of 1936. After the success of the Hanna House, begun some three years previously, Wright continued to explore the possibilities of the hexagonal shape, as he believed that it offered greater spatial freedom than the rectangle of the previous Usonians and enabled him to "break the box" still further. For Wright, the hexagon, and eventually, and logically, the circle was more natural and "organic" in terms of human movement. Certainly the hexagonal form gives an entirely different feeling for internal and external space from a rectangular module. The Bazett House walls and axes are at 60 and 120 degree

Right: Exterior of living room. The ingenious plan of the house allows the living room windows to face both into the "L" of the construction on one side and out into the valley and bay on the opposite side. The broad overhang of the eaves protects what is virtually a glass curtain of windows against extremes of sunlight.

Right: Living room interior, showing dining area, hearth, and workspace. The floor-to-ceiling windows and doors on the private side of the house form what is virtually a glass curtain wall on to the terrace.

Right: Living room interior with seating area. Although compact in size, less than 1,500 square feet, the house is ingeniously designed to appear more spacious with a high paneled ceiling and a continuous run of perforated panels forming clerestory windows at ceiling level.

angles, like those of the Hanna House, although it was originally more compact and Wright was to alter and expand it from its original conception for later owners. The flexibility and organic nature of the Usonian form, and especially of the hexagonal, allowed Wright to progressively expand the original design, ingeniously increasing the living spaces, despite the original house's relatively small size and compactness. The house was completed in its present form in the mid 1950s.

The most distinctive internal feature of the house is still the original living room space, which is joined to the bedroom wing at an angle of 60 degrees. As the room is set, it commands a view of the valley and the bay in the distance as well as views out onto the terrace and into the "L" of the inward-looking space. The distinctive floor-to-ceiling fenestration on the private side of the house takes the form of an angled glass curtain wall, while, in contrast, privacy is maintained on the "public" façade by a series of clerestory windows of unique design formed of fretwork redwood batten. The use of clerestory windows, high enough to guarantee the owners' privacy while allowing light to filter through, is a distinctive feature of the Usonian interior, one adapted from Wright's earlier work, previously seen at its most distinctive in the Californian textile block houses. The high-set windows diffuse the light and cast interesting and changing shadows—a characteristic feature of Usonian houses, and one long remembered by their owners. The same redwood is used throughout the house for walls and ceilings and for the characteristic Usonian built-in furnishing, and, true to Wright's principles, the focal point of the living space is a large angled brick fireplace of distinctive design. Externally the house is distinguished by the steep overhang of the gables of its roof, appropriate for the Californian climate. Wright, perhaps looking back to the Prairie houses of the first period of his success, provides broad overhangs that cast deep shadows and offer protection from bright light, making practicable the floor-to-ceiling screen of windows on the garden side of the house.

Above: Living room interior with terrace beyond. A continuous run of built-in seating is topped by a run of shelving and display space beneath a band of clerestory windows of alternate cut-out boards and clear glass.

Wright conceived the design of the Administration Building as an inward-looking "sealed space," in which the radical use of glass tube walls made it impossible for the workers to see the outside world, and the industrial activity that surrounded it. In its solution to a complex problem, the building is reminiscent of Wright's early work of 1904, the Larkin Administration Building, which had been dedicated to what the architect described as the "unpopular gospel of work." A key difference, 32 years later, is the fact that the sheer concrete walls and top-lighting of the Larkin Building are replaced by walls of light diffused through glass tubes. Wright wrote of the Johnson complex, "Organic architecture designed this great building to be as inspiring a place to work as any cathedral ever was in which to worship," and the analogy is made clearer both by the height of the building and in its use of glass to flood the interior.

The administrative office of 1936–39 demonstrated Wright's skill in devising inward-looking spaces most dramatically, perhaps, in the tour-de-force of the space of the central workroom where daylight is diffused through rows of Pyrex glass tubes providing an interior, which effectively shuts off the outside world to the workers within it, as it is impossible to see through the tubed glass screens that both refract and diffuse the light. The effect is further enhanced by the graceful concrete

Right: Detail of tubed screen wall. While the innovative use of Pyrex tubes enabled Wright to achieve his purpose of diffusing and refracting natural light, as well as providing insulation, they were also elegant and minimalistic, providing a unique style and design for the building.

Right: Interior showing the concrete "lily pad" columns and the advanced Pyrex tube technology that enables the windowless interior to become a space filled with diffused daylight.

100

columns that are reminiscent of huge lily pads. The tunnel vaulted pedestrian bridge and the reception area of the publicity department are also formed of circular Pyrex glass tubes, which achieve Wright's purpose of both diffusing natural light and providing insulation. In addition, the tubed windows provided elegant and minimalist decorative opportunities.

The only drawback to the use of such radical technology lay in the manner in which the tubes were prone to leaking, before a clear silicone caulking process was invented. It was said that even Johnson's own office was not immune from leakage, and that he kept a trash can near his desk to catch the drips when necessary. Modern waterproof adhesives have since replaced the originals. Such workaday considerations apart, the effect from both the interior and exterior is streamlined and of the moment. The building also rescued Wright's flagging financial fortunes and brought him back into the public eye with the sheer amount of publicity it provoked.

In *An Autobiography* published in 1944, Wright gives his own verdict on the building:

> "To enumerate in detail or even catalog the innovations to be found in this one building would require more time and patient attention on your part, and mine too, than either of us cares to give it. So let's say here that it is technically, and in the entire realm of the scientific art of Architecture, one of the world's most remarkable structures. I like it. They like it. Let it go at that."

Right: Interior view of the tunnel vaulted pedestrian bridge linking the publicity department and the executive department. The use of Pyrex glass was radical at the time, diffusing and refracting the light as well as providing insulation.

Left: Detail of tubed screen wall, showing the joints of the circular Pyrex tubes. Lumiline bulbs were inserted between two layers of glass tubing to illuminate the building at night by diffusing electric light, simulating the effect of sunlight.

LIGHTING

SUSAN LAWRENCE DANA (DANA-THOMAS) HOUSE,
TALIESIN LAMP, THE "GLASS-LESS LIGHT," V.C. MORRIS
GIFT SHOP.

3

The designs for lighting fixtures and

fittings that Wright produced from the earliest years of his practice as an architect are an integral part of his ideal of an organic architecture in which the design of every detail in the house was an essential part of the whole. Writing on his work with electric lighting in 1928, he stated that lighting was "no longer an appliance nor even an appurtenance, but really architecture…made a part of the building…I can see limitless possibilities of beauty in this one feature of the use of glass."

His most distinctive designs using glass were achieved in the Oak Park years when electric lighting became a new and exciting force in the everyday life of those who could afford the luxury of their own electric generator, long before electricity became generally available through the grid system. Wright responded to the challenges of new technology throughout his life, and the use of electricity in both the private and the public domain was no exception. Indeed, his interest in, and experience of, the unprecedented opportunities offered by

Above right: Henry Allen House, Wichita, KS. Interior of living room showing the double row of wooden-framed fretwork ceiling light grilles that extend the length of the room. The light was diffused through the grilles by means of rice paper.

Right: Warren McArthur House, Chicago, Illinois. Lamp fixture on the newel post of the staircase. A simple, lantern-based design, in contrast to the elaborate art glass of the dining room of the house.

Right: Herbert F. Johnson House "Wingspread," Wind Point, WI. Floor lamp and chair. Wingspread, one of the largest and most expensive domestic commission of Wright's career, contains several unique fittings, including this floor lamp of rectilinear design.

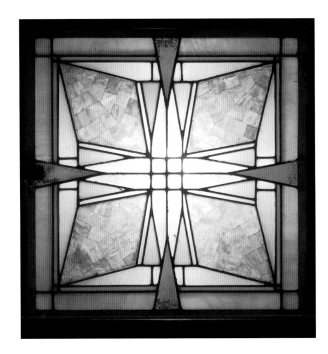

Above: Frank Thomas House, Oak Park, Illinois. Entry ceiling light. The fixture uses the arrowhead motif seen in the art glass throughout the house. Mother of pearl tesserae are used to form a shimmering mosaic.

Right: Frank Thomas House. Entrance vestibule. The entrance doors and windows, together with the light fixture above the door, all use the same arrowhead motif, making this a completely integrated ensemble.

electricity may be traced to his apprentice years. Two years before Wright's marriage, when he first came to Chicago in 1887, the city was in the midst of the building boom that had followed the Great Fire of 1871. Wright's apprenticeship to Louis Sullivan, whom he was to term his "Lieber Meister" for the rest of his life, was undertaken during the period in which Sullivan and his partner, Dankmar Adler, were working on the Auditorium Building, a building that epitomized the aesthetic and technological dynamism that distinguished turn-of-the-nineteenth-century Chicago.

The new technologies were transforming modern buildings: the economical production of rolled plate glass, for example, was used for the first fully glazed curtain wall façade in Chicago in 1895 for the Brunswick (Studebaker) Building by S.S. Berman. Thomas Alva Edison's carbon-filament incandescent lamp was used in the extraordinarily elaborate lighting schemes of Adler and Sullivan's Auditorium Theater and, by the late nineties, in the domestic domain.

Sullivan and Adler made their reputation with the great public buildings of downtown Chicago. The Auditorium Building was the heaviest (at 110,000 tons) and most massive modern building in the world, when it was opened in 1889. Technologically it was extraordinarily advanced for its time: the most fireproofed building ever constructed and the first large scale building to be electrically lit and air-conditioned. The spectacular auditorium, which seats 4,200, is distinguished by its superb acoustics (a factor that was to stand Wright in good stead when he came to design auditoria in later life: he was to describe it as "the greatest room for music and opera in the world bar none") and by its use of electric light. The great arched ceiling of the theater is illuminated by thousands of carbon filament bulbs, conceived as part of the overall floriated design. The light cast is soft and flattering, complementing the elaborate decoration of the whole spectacular *mise-en-scéne* of the interior. Throughout Wright's career he was to prefer recessed lighting that was integral to the architecture, and this was learned from his apprenticeship with Adler and Sullivan on the Auditorium building, together with overhead illumination, as in nature.

With the success of the Auditorium Building, Sullivan and Adler, who preferred to work on large commercial structures, began the process of giving smaller domestic commissions to their chief draftsman, Frank Lloyd Wright. It is possible to see in the work on the renovations and additions carried out on his own house at Oak Park, which were begun in 1895, how Wright transformed what he had learned as Sullivan's apprentice in to a radically new style. Nowhere is this more evident than in the transformation of the foliage design motifs from the Auditorium Building into the lighting designs at Oak Park.

Sullivan had sought to articulate ornament through stylized organic forms, as evidenced in the lighting fixtures of the Auditorium Building. Wright, however, even at this early stage of his career, emphasized the geometrical relationships that can be seen to underlie all structures. The striking design for the ceiling grille, above the dining table in the house at Oak Park, demonstrates both the advances made in Wright's lighting design and the influence of Sullivan. The design of the cut-out panel combines several forms of decoration in a complex whole. These range from stylized oak leaves at the outer edges, which closely follow

Sullivan's ornamental motifs, to the strict geometry of the four large circular motifs. The lighting fitments themselves are not on open display unlike those of the bulbs and glass shades of the Auditorium Building that form an integral part of the design scheme, but recessed and set into the ceiling behind the fretwork ceiling grille.

This feature was much admired in the progressive women's magazine, *House Beautiful* of February 1897. In an article entitled "Successful Homes," the writer is particularly enthusiastic about the lighting grille: "Great ingenuity has been used in the arrangement of the electric light...There is not a bulb in sight, but let into the ceiling and actually part of it, is a screen of intricate pattern, covered with thin paper. The light is turned on above and filters through much subdued." This last was a particularly important feature for domestic lighting. In England the satirical magazine *Punch* published a cartoon in 1889 showing the

Above: Frank Lloyd Wright Home and Studio, Oak Park, Illinois. Illuminated fretwork ceiling grille above the dining table. The forms of the design are curvilinear and incorporate oak leaves. The earliest example of Wright's use of an electrically illuminated "light screen." it was intended to give the effect of sunlight filtering through leaves.

Right: Henry Allen House, Wichita. Floor lamp with stand. This lamp continues the Japanese theme so much in evidence in other features of the design of the house, with its rectilinear forms and translucent shade like a miniature pagoda.

disadvantages of the new electric lighting, with a group of ladies listening to a recital in a fashionable salon with Japanese parasols raised against the bright light, while a servant holds a parasol to protect the singer and her music. One of the earliest English writers on electricity, Mrs. J. E. H. Gordon, in her *Decorative Electricity with a Chapter on Fire Risks* published in 1891, went further in her advice for lighting the modern home: "There was a round table seating ten guests, and ten lamps with lemon yellow shades were hung just above their eyes, so that the light focused into the eyes and face of everyone sitting at table...showing every wrinkle and line in the face. No one over the age of eighteen should be asked to sit beneath such a light!"

Wright's solution to this problem was to diffuse the light by filtering it through rice paper, which had the effect of dappled sunlight, while the whole elaborate form was made possible by the lowering of the ceiling to accommodate it. Wright was to develop the device in later ceiling light screens with bulbs set behind art glass for his Prairie house commissions and in the fretwork panels of the Usonian houses.

The use of electricity to turn night into day in such a controlled and dramatic manner may be seen as part of a wider philosophy of the idea of the unifying force of home and family life current in the United States at the time. In 1896–97, Wright provided the decorative designs and assisted in the publication of an influential book by a Unitarian Minister, William C. Gannett, which extolled the ideal house as a site that "should be home for all our parts. Eyes and ears are eager to be fed with harmonies in color and form and sound; these are their natural food as much as bread and meat are food for other parts." Indeed it might be argued that the style and design of Wright's domestic interiors throughout his life, long after he had left his family and home at Oak Park, would seem to conform to this utopian ideal of his early years as an architect. Light, either in the form of the natural daylight, which was his ideal throughout his career, or as "artificial sunshine", as the early advocates of electric lighting were to call it, plays a key part in his organic interiors.

Wright's use of top-lighting, whether in the form of clerestory windows, skylights, or grilles illuminated by electricity, is a key feature of

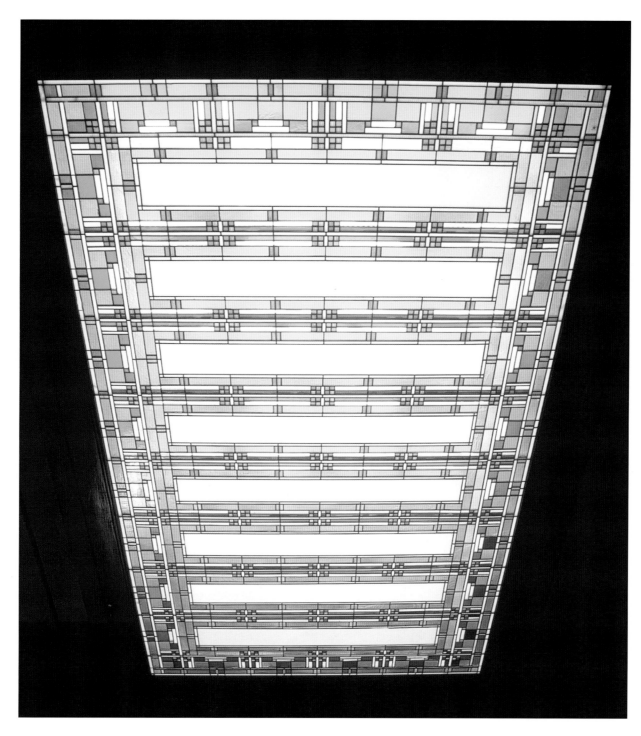

Left: Frank Lloyd Wright Home and Studio, Oak Park, Illinois. Studio sky-light. One of the most dramatic of Wright's lighting designs, the colors and squared and rectilinear design form an abstract glass "picture" in the ceiling, set as it is in deeply recessed wooden framed panels.

the remodeled house and studio of 1895. John Lloyd Wright, in his recollections of his childhood home, recalls rooms where "lights filtered through fret-sawed ceiling grilles," and such a grille was also part of the top-lighting of the lofty, barrel-vaulted playroom of John Lloyd Wright and his five siblings' childhood.

Among these additions and renovations, it can be seen that Wright used top-lighting for different purposes, particularly in the working spaces of the house. The intricate art-glass skylight of the studio reception room in which clients and contractors were received, is not simply an integrated decorative feature, but also serves the purpose of linking the drafting room, Wright's own office, and the library. Light is diffused through a tapestry-like design of gold, sage, and amber art glass, off-set with an occasional pattern of clear glass. The Sullivan-like forms of the earlier dining room grille are transformed here into a decorative form that diffuses light, as well as refracting it during the day and also forms what might be regarded as a framed glass abstract "picture" in the ceiling, set as it is in deeply recessed wooden-framed panels.

Art-glass skylights are also used to open the ceiling space and illuminate the interior at Unity Temple, Wright's most significant public building of the Oak Park years. The panels are protected on the exterior by a glass shell and each of the panels, recessed into the ceiling, is made up of an integrated and organic but subtly varied design using art-glass motifs set into oak frames, the whole forming an extraordinary canopy of diffused gold light that illuminates the entire central space.

The light fittings of Unity Temple are a radical departure in Wright's work. Four splendid lighting fixtures formed of spherical glass globes and glass cubes, which recall the Froebel Gifts of Wright's childhood, hang beneath the height of the gallery from cantilevered supports. The glass globes form a counterpoint to the overall rectilinear of the design in a manner that would be used in later designs, notably those of the Robie House. The cords of the fixtures are exposed, indeed drawn attention to, by the gold silk thread that covers them. True to Arts and Crafts principles of truth to materials, the true nature of the electrical fitting is made clear and its radical departure from gas lighting made apparent, as the forms chosen would be impossible to achieve with the

older technology. Wright held strongly to the opinion that new technologies should not be used to replicate old styles of design, but used in conjunction with the machine to create fresh concepts and to express modernity.

The purity and simplicity of the geometric shapes of the lighting fixtures at Unity Temple are in marked contrast to the lighting Wright designed for the homes of his clients at Oak Park, River Forest, and Springfield of the period. As with the furniture designed for particular houses, Wright's designs for lighting fixtures were site-specific, and here too Wright used the latest technology to explore new solutions and possibilities, while adhering to the principles of organic architecture.

In *In the Cause of Architecture* (1908), he writes of the importance of a "certain simple form" that "characterizes the expression of one building" and cites the example of the Dana Thomas House, "from one basic idea of the formal elements of design are in each case derived and held well together in scale and character...its grammar may be

Right: Unity Temple, Oak Park, Illinois. Temple interior showing the light fixtures, which are formed of solid translucent spheres, cubes, and squares. The gold and amber tones of the whole interior extend to the detail of the gold silk that covers the wiring of the lamps.

deduced from some plant form that has appealed to me, as certain properties in line and form of the sumac were used in the Lawrence house…each building aesthetically is cut from one piece of goods and consistently hangs together with an integrity impossible otherwise."

The Dana House has a particularly elaborate variety of light fixtures and fittings, but other houses of the Oak Park years, the Darwin Martin House for example, also have some remarkable lighting designs. Indirect lighting continued to be Wright's favorite form of illumination, and recessed lighting, often at ceiling height, is a constant feature of his later work, as it had been from his earliest experiments with forms of electric lighting. The soft, diffused quality of such lighting helped achieve the quality of repose he sought in all his interiors.

In Wright's final Prairie house designs the lighting was integrated into the overall scheme of the house to achieve further assimilation with the whole design, whether it was the repeating rectilinear forms of the ceiling light and lighting fixtures of the Meyer May House of 1910, or the geometric accents of the lighting that complements and integrates the various constituent parts of the overall scheme of the Robie House. The design of the art-glass ceiling lights of the living room of the May residence is an elegant and refined variation on a theme begun with the dining room grille of his own house at Oak Park. Here the artificial light is filtered, not through rice-paper but subtly toned art glass formed of the geometrical shapes seen in the art-glass windows throughout the house. As is often the case in such schemes, the design

Above: Darwin D. Martin House, Buffalo, New York. Dining room showing lighting fixtures. The dominant geometric form of the glass design of the room is that of the rectangle. The ceiling light and art-glass windows, and the doors of the sideboard, use a "tree of life" motif.

Above: Sophie and Meyer May Residence, Grand Rapids, Michigan. Art-glass lamp fixture and windows with a set of Froebel blocks. The Meyer May house, fully restored in the 1980s is exceptionally integrated in its glass and lighting designs. The geometric forms of the blocks, so crucial to Wright's work, can be seen in both lamp and window.

Above right: Sophie and Meyer May Residence. Living room illuminated light screens and windows. A series of ceiling light screens, of similar rectilinear design to the windows illuminates the room from above, an elegant variation on a theme begun with the grille of Wright's dining room at Oak Park.

of the ceiling light is more complex than that of the other glasswork in the space, deeper in hue and more abstract in its motifs. In the living room, the ceiling lights are rhymed with a wall of art-glass windows and complemented by lamps, which are fixed to occupy a specific space as part of the whole luminous and harmonious composition.

The designs for the Robie House were particularly influential in both the United States and Europe. A photograph of the dining room of the Robie House in Chicago soon after it was completed in 1910 shows the extraordinary control Wright exerted over the integration of every element of his designs into a total environment. Built-in lamps or *torchères* illuminate the four corners of the dining table, their glass shades reflect the forms of the art-glass window designs. The rectilinear forms of the whole ensemble, from table and chairs to the built-in sideboard and carpet pattern are off set and punctuated by the glass globes of the ceiling light fixtures, which form the terminal points of the wooden bands of paneling that run across the ceiling. The sophistication and elegance of the Robie House dining room represents the culmination of Wright's desire that light fixtures should be "made a part of the building…no longer an appliance nor even an appurtenance, but really architecture."

His client, Frederick C. Robie, had trained as an engineer, and was president of a bicycle manufacturing company. He had very distinct

ideas about the nature of the house he wanted, which had to be fireproof with open vistas within and privacy from his neighbors. When he first met Wright in 1906, Robie remembered "When I talked in mechanical terms, he talked in architectural terms. I thought, well, he was in my world." The designs were published widely and the spherical glass and bronze lighting fixtures throughout the house were especially admired, particularly as they, in common with the other specially designed features of the house, appeared distinctively streamlined and modern. Wright was especially pleased with the fact that in Germany "the house became known as 'Dampfer' (ocean liner architecture); it was a good example of the prairie house of that period. This further emphasized that the machine could be a tool in the hands of the artist."

There are echoes of the Robie House table illumination in the distinctive light fixture designed for the living room of the Aline Barnsdall ("Hollyhock") House. In keeping with the overall abstracted flower motifs used throughout each element of the house, Wright used the hollyhock motifs carved into seven foot high *torchères* to complete the dramatic ensemble around the hearth of the living room. The lamps are set in angled tables at the ends of the sofa and their soft light is directed toward the ceiling from upturned glass pyramids. The subtle lighting arrangement of the room is further enhanced, in typical Wrightian fashion, by concealed recessed lighting that runs around the room at ceiling height. In this, the last of Wright's dramatic lighting ensembles, a further reference to his past designs may be seen in the fretwork skylight grille which rises diagonally above the dramatic "sacred hearth", formed from similar stylized hollyhock motifs as the lamp fixtures and those repeated throughout the entire design of this remarkable house.

Fretwork grilles and recessed lighting were to continue to appear in Wright's work, albeit in more modest forms. The Usonian houses employed both devices, often as their only decorative details. The Pope Leighey House, for example, used perforated panels at ceiling height to allow different patterns of light into the interior, a device first used in the Californian textile block houses, most dramatically perhaps in the Storer House in Los Angeles. In the Usonians, such as the Pope Leighey House, the same design of perforated cypress board panels was used

ingeniously throughout the house. The panels, made of glass between half-inch board, could be opened at clerestory level to provide ventilation. Sometimes they were placed horizontally, as in the clerestory lights, sometimes vertically as in the bedrooms, where half panels were put together to create the effect of shutters. Clients were asked to suggest motifs and in the case of the clerestory windows of the Charles Weltzheimer House (1948) in Oberlin, Ohio, Wright used a circular design to evoke, it appears, the apple trees on the site.

The house built for Lowell and Agnes Walter ("Cedar Rock") on a spectacular site in Quasqueton, Iowa, followed Usonian principles to a marked degree. What might be termed light screens were used both externally and internally but without the usual patterned perforations. A generous budget for both house and fixtures rendered the space far more extensive and expensively appointed than usual and it was built on a spectacular site in a wooded valley that would be far beyond the means of the average Usonian owner. The use of glass in the building is

Above: "Hollyhock House," Los Angeles, California. Living room with lamp fixtures and ceiling light screen. The two large wooden standard lamps are set into the sofa tables providing uplighting. Their design echoes the dominant hollyhock motif of the entire house.

Left: Harold C. Price Tower, Bartlesville, Oklahoma. Interior of Mr Price's office with hanging lamp and mural designed by Wright. The spiky angularity of the design elements of the room, seen in the mural and "dentist's chair," are also seen in the pendant lamp.

Left: Frank Thomas House, Oak Park, Ill. Exterior lantern on the newel post of the stair leading to the vestibule of the house, which can be seen in the background.

Left: Beth Sholom Synagogue, Elkins Park, PA. View of the interior showing the central "wings" feature. The light-filled translucent glass interior is built to a triangular module. The brilliantly illuminated stained glass central chandelier echoes this dominant motif.

unique in a Wright domestic building, with three glass walls and a series of skylights providing the means whereby the aptly named garden room, the main living room of the house is able to sustain a sizeable interior planting. The exterior of the house is distinguished by a reinforced concrete roof with broad cantilevered overhangs with upturned edges, which are pierced as a form of trellis. This has the effect of shading the extensive areas of window glass from bright sunlight, while the under-floor gravity heating, common to Usonian designs, is here laid in independent segments for the plantings, so that any fault could be immediately located and dealt with.

Wright's largest public building, the huge Marin County Civic Center, also contains a spectacular planting at its heart, lit by a series of light wells and huge continuous skylights. Wright received the commission for the vast complex in 1957 and presented his plans just under a year later. The spectacular site, which spans three hills and accommodates the county offices, the courts of justice, the central library, the jail and other civic spaces, remained unfinished at the time of Wright's death in 1959.

Wright's public buildings of his late career include such diverse commissions as the Beth Sholom Synagogue and the Solomon Guggenheim Museum, New York. The Synagogue is conceived as a huge translucent pyramid-like form, completely free of internal support and roofed translucently—Wright referred to the structure as "a lighted mountain." The softly diffused light of the interior is contrasted to the central "wings" feature of brilliantly illuminated stained glass in resonant symbolic colors, in which the pyramidal forms repeat the basic triangle of the design module that informs the whole structure, from the ground plan itself to the integrated ornament.

For the lighting of the Solomon Guggenheim Museum, Wright revisited the radical Pyrex tube technology he had used in the S. C.

Johnson Administrative Building. Wright believed that paintings and works of art were best experienced in the changing conditions of natural light, preferably from above as top-lighting, a truth to which most of the great galleries of the world attest. Wright's solution to the problem of lighting the entire museum was intended to replicate natural light as far as possible. Daylight floods into the ivory space through the monumental hemispherical dome, the key to the whole "skyward" expansion of the great central space. The radical glass-tube technology used in the Johnson Wax Administration Building was developed in the design for the original skylights or "rifts", which run the entire length of the internal ramp on its outer edge, enclosing a system of incandescent tubes that subtly enhance the natural flow of light.

On a lesser scale, the V.C. Morris Gift Shop in San Francisco, of 1948–49, has a spiral interior and is often perceived as a forerunner of the Guggenheim on a small scale. The spiral form of the defining ramp of the interior, which extends through the two stories of the shop, is echoed in the circular forms that abound elsewhere in the design—from the illuminated niches that hold the goods for sale to the hemispherical dome of the ceiling with its striking clusters of domed light fixtures. The dark, cavern-like entrance to the shop gives no indication of what lies within, although attention is subtly drawn to the arched opening by the horizontal and vertical lights set into the brickwork of the defining wall and the façade, which is entirely without windows. This feature of the design is antithetical to the plate glass display windows that still constituted the norm of shop display in the middle of the twentieth century, 50 years after Wright's mentor, Louis Sullivan, had designed the Carson Pirie Scott store in Chicago, which became the model for spectacular shop windows designed to attract shoppers to the goods inside.

CASE STUDY: SUSAN LAWRENCE DANA (DANA-THOMAS) HOUSE

SUSAN LAWRENCE DANA (DANA-THOMAS) HOUSE,
SPRINGFIELD, ILLINOIS. CONSTRUCTED 1902.

In 1908, in *In the Cause of Architecture* Wright wrote of the importance of "a single, certain simple form" that "characterizes the expression of one building" and cites the example of the Dana-Thomas House "from one basic idea all the formal elements of design are in each case derived and held well together in scale and character."

In fact, the Dana-Thomas House, the best preserved and most complete example of Wright's design aesthetic of the Prairie Style years, uses a number of motifs in its design, one of which is that of butterfly wings.

Wright identified the hanging lamps of the Dana dining room as "butterfly lamps" and according to an advertisement in *The Architectural Record* of March, 1908, the fixtures were made by the Linden Glass Company of Chicago, as well as the art glass of the house. The lamp is of complex design and is constructed of hundreds of precision-cut pieces: a series of planes and angles make up the stylized "butterfly" forms and the design employs various types of glass: sandblasted, clear, colored and iridescent in its making.

No less complex in form are the many table lamps that were also made by the Linden Glass Company. The design of these lamps, variations on which can be seen throughout the house, are distinctly oriental and evoke Japanese motifs derived from the prints of Wright's own

Above right: Hanging "butterfly" lamp. The lamps, measuring nearly two feet in width and some 33 inches on the diagonal are designed to be of interest from whichever angle they are viewed. The forms of the art glass suggest butterflies at rest, while the hangers are articulated with square block-like forms. Other blocks add interest to the shade from below.

Right: Fountain light fixture. Wright's love of subdued, subtle lighting effects can be seen in the dark tonalities of the art glass used to light the space. The color harmonies and patterns of the art-glass lights echo the glass screen and doors of the fountain space as a whole.

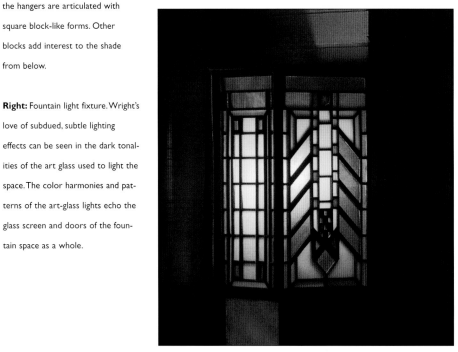

Right: Studio light fitments. In the studio, the vaulted space has a wide shelf running in front of art-glass windows, from which the ribs of the vault spring. Along this shelf are ranged a row of standing art-glass lamps, sharing a similar rectilinear pattern with the windows. Wall-mounted lamps, more attenuated in form, are ranged behind them to provide rich and subdued lighting for the space.

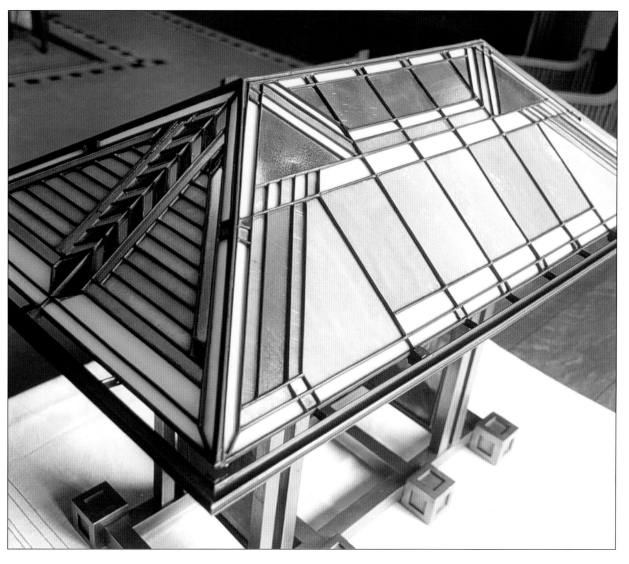

Left: The brass base supports a complex shade formed of electroplated gilt zinc cames. Both the tonalities of the glass and the abstracted forms of the sumac plant that make up its design are seen throughout the house.

collection, which were a key factor in his work and an important constituent of the design vocabulary of the Prairie house. The design of the table lamps throughout the house is perhaps the most overt Japanese reference in all his designs for lighting, recalling both Japanese paper parasols and the steep overhang of pagoda roofs.

The sixteen-sided shades of the single pedestal lamps are made of paneled glass with electroplated gilt zinc cames on a brass base, irides-

cent and colored glass are used in both shade and base. Other lamps in the house elaborate on the Japanese theme, the most remarkable of which is the design for a double pedestal lamp. This recalls, in its angularity, a miniature Japanese temple (or perhaps a miniature Prairie house) with a steeply overhanging roof, rather than the parasol-like forms seen in the single-pedestal lamps.

Here, too, the design motif of the shade is different and more

Left: Double pedestal lamp. One of Wright's most elegant lighting designs, this recalls a miniature Japanese pagoda. The color harmonies of green, gold, and yellow echo those found throughout the house, while the iridescent glass panels of the supports offset the distinctive patina of the bronze frame.

Right: Entry ceiling light seen from below. The repeating geometrical motifs of the design echo that of the external frieze, as well as the abstracted sumac design seen elsewhere in the ornament of the house.

closely integrated with the abstracted sumac forms of the interior design features. The iridescent glass panels beneath the shade rest on hinged supports, while the color harmonies, of green and gold, echo the autumnal tones of the rest of the house, from the art-glass shade to the patina of the bronze base. The glass furnishings of the Dana House represent Wright's most elaborate and expensive ensemble of such work,

ranging from hanging ceiling lights and wall sconces, table lamps and even a set of floor lights in the grand entrance to the house, behind the "Flower in the Crannied Wall" sculpture. The library is illuminated by no less than 15 horizontal wall lights, mounted on beams and eight identical vertically mounted fittings on the wood-finished piers, in addition to several table lamps.

Left: Butterfly lamp seen from below. The dramatic pendant lighting fixtures present sophisticated views from every angle. The pools of golden light produced by the lamps are given added interest from below by the paired square blocks that articulate the base of the rectilinear design of the lamp. The entire fitment shows Wright's adaptation of the latest technology to his overall design purpose.

Right: Entry-way lamp seen from above. The parasol-like standing lamp is raised on a high pedestal to cast a subdued light in the space, which includes the "Flower on the Crannied Wall" sculpture . The geometric pattern and green and gold coloration of the glass echo the ornament and decoration elsewhere in the space.

Left: Single wall-mounted lamp. These lamps are used in subtle variants, wall-mounted, or free-standing, throughout the house to provide the subdued back-lighting effects so crucial to Wright's style and design ethos.

CASE STUDY: TALIESIN LAMP

One of Wright's best known and most widely copied lighting designs is for the so-called "Taliesin lamp." The wooden and paper lamps may be seen in a variety of interiors. First used at Taliesin, Wright's Wisconsin home, they evoke the materials, if not the form, of his earliest experiments with electric lighting in the dining room fixture of his first home at Oak Park. The house had only been electrified in 1891, but when, four years later, Wright was able to extend the house and studio, his designs for the dining room included an extraordinary fretwork screen above the central dining table that diffused the light through rice paper. This had the effect of softening the light and hiding the unsightly bulbs that had, in the early years of electricity at least, a decidedly unflattering glare, especially when above a dining table. The Oak Park light screen had the effect of filtering the light, illuminating the table, as Wright wrote, "as sunlight sifts through leaves in the trees."

Thirty years later, Wright looked back to wood and paper as the organic components of a pedestal-based table lamp or a floor-standing standard. The light is softly diffused through a paper or cloth shade, which is contained in tapered wooden ribs and raised on a wooden base. The whole design is emphatically Japanese in its inspiration, recalling Wright's work on the Imperial Hotel in Tokyo. It may also be said to recall the steep overhang of the Prairie house designs in its overall shape. However, the simplicity and functionality of the design, and its use of simple organic materials, is in striking contrast to the extravagance and elaboration of the Dana-Thomas House double pedestal lamps, whose shape it distantly recalls and which derive from the same Japanese-inspired sources.

The light is diffused through a paper or cloth shade, and the original Taliesin version is a play upon square motifs, from the square base and square shade to the small wooden square at the top, which provides space and air for the light socket. The ribs of the shade taper and, as with the Oak Park fixture, the bulb is completely concealed by the shade.

Wright had used cantilevered lamps at Midway Gardens a decade before and looked back to these prototype lamps for later lighting

Right: Don and Virginia Lovness House, Stillwater, Minnesota. Living room lamps used to illuminate the seating area. The lamps can be table or wall mounted, or, as here, built into the sofa-tables to provide additional sources of light.

designs, including the bedside lamps at Taliesin and the many adaptations he designed as living room fixtures for the houses of clients who admired the design.

None of the Midway Gardens lamps survive, but photographs, and Wright's original drawings, showed that the lamp was adjustable, with the cantilevered shade support that could be raised and lowered above the dining tables in the Winter Gardens of Midway Gardens. The octagonal glass shade of the lamp was made of opaque glass.

A variation on these Midway Gardens lamps may be seen in the built-in light fixtures in the living room of a house designed for Donald and Virginia Lovness in Stillwater, Minnesota, in 1955, which is built on a simple four-foot module. The house was built by the owners to Wright's design and the square module, which defines and integrates the entire design, is repeated in the lighting throughout the house—from the recessed downlights to the wooden light fixtures.

Left: Don and Virginia Lovness House, Stillwater, Minnesota. View of main living area showing the lighting of the space. Daylight, from the floor-to-ceiling windows on the private side of the house, is enhanced by a continuous run of downlighters set into the paneling and by clerestory windows above. Key areas of the room are subtly lit by Taliesin lamps.

Wright's designs for Midway Gardens (the European style entertainment complex that was opened in 1914, declared bankrupt within two years, and finally demolished in 1929) were extraordinarily innovatory; "a festival for the eyes," as Wright described it. The vast complex, in downtown Chicago, integrated architecture, sculpture, landscape design, ceramics, murals, and furniture in an ambitious enterprise that could seat some 700 people in an open-air complex with room for dancing and various forms of entertainment. The integrating design motifs throughout were geometric. Used in such elements as the murals, ceramics, and furniture, the geometric forms and bright primary colors recall the Froebel blocks of Wright's childhood and, indeed, in "The City by the Sea" murals, the balloon shapes and parade theme of the Coonley Playhouse windows of two years before.

The overall emphasis in Midway Gardens, as with all Wright's designs for both public and private spaces of the time was horizontal. To counter this horizontality, Wright introduced various vertical elements, including distinctive sculptures, tall spires, and sculptural forms. The lighting fixtures were also vertical in emphasis and photographs of sculptures by Alfonso Iannelli in the Summer Garden are shown to be placed on brick plinths alongside glass and metal lights with designs reminiscent of the sculptures in their block-like forms. One of Wright's drawings for the lighting fixture of the Garden Terrace lamps shows front and side elevations for these lamps, which were made of bronze on concrete bases. Using sandblasted opaque glass with red-glass accents, they were topped by finials of bronze cubes. Basic geometric forms were used throughout the lighting of the varied spaces of the complex, extending to the detail of the cords of the Winter Gardens lighting fixtures, which were hung with tiny spheres and cubes.

The so called "glass-less light" is obviously derived from this Midway Gardens design, although it uses wood and not bronze, and is able, because it is designed to be used as part of an interior, to eliminate the opaque glass cubes that concealed the bulbs of the original structure. The sculptural qualities of the design remain, however, and the hanging versions as well as the floor and table standing types are

Right: Herbert and Katherine Jacobs First residence, Madison, Wisconsin. The glass-less light illuminates an otherwise unlit corner of the room. The rectangular module, which determines the entire design, may also be seen in the paneling, the mullions of the windows, and in the scored pattern on the concrete floor pad.

Right: Herbert and Katherine Jacobs First Residence, Madison, Wisconsin. Living room with glassless light seen as a corner fixture. A sense of space in a small area is created by streamlining essential components, and, wherever possible, building them into the design, as in this, the first Usonian house.

designed to work as pieces of wooden sculpture when unlit. The bulbs are placed in wooden boxes at reversed angles around the central post, while reflectors direct the light downward. The reflectors could be adapted according to where the light was to be placed. Those designed to be placed on a table or built into a wall, as with the fitting that forms a focal point in the living room of the Jacobs House, for example, used reflecting shades, which were placed above and below to direct the light where needed.

The Jacobs House, near Madison, Wisconsin, was the first of the Usonian houses to be designed and constructed in 1936. It is built to a two-by-four foot rectangular module. The rectangular unit is scored into the concrete floor pad and the motif repeated in the forms of the paneling and the windows. Light is brought into the public side of the house by the use of clerestory windows, while the windows to the terrace and garden form a floor-to-ceiling glass screen. The recess formed by the brick walls of the living room is a nook that receives little daylight. The built-in glass-less light thus has both function and aesthetic purpose.

The glass-less light was made from different woods according to purpose and size required—the Jacobs light, which is floor-mounted, differs from the table-top versions, such as that at Taliesin. The Lovness house, in Stillwater, Minnesota, of 1955, has a double variant of the glass-less light to illuminate its dining table. The square motifs that form the lights perfectly complement the square module that defines and integrates the entire design of the house.

CASE STUDY: V.C. MORRIS GIFT SHOP

V.C. MORRIS GIFT SHOP, SAN FRANCISCO,
CALIFOR-NIA. CONSTRUCTED IN 1948.

In 1948 Wright was to return to California after a space of 30 years. The projects achieved in his last decade there were very different from his earlier domestic commissions, the California Romanza. Both were public buildings, the monumental Marin County Civic center, San Rafael, California, is the major California project of his last decade and was completed after his death. In contrast, the tiny V. C. Morris Gift Shop in the center of San Francisco was begun in 1948 and completed within the year.

The dark, cave-like entrance to the shop gives no indication of what lies within, although, particularly at night, attention is drawn to the arched opening by the horizontal and vertical lights set into the brick-work, and even in daylight the shop lights can be glimpsed through the horizontal spaces that form part of the design. The site of the shop is a narrow one, and Wright turns this to advantage by accentuating the theatrical entrance arch, which is both reminiscent of a Roman tunnel vault and recalls the "Richardsonian Romanesque" style of Henry Hobson Richardson, an architect whose domestic and public buildings

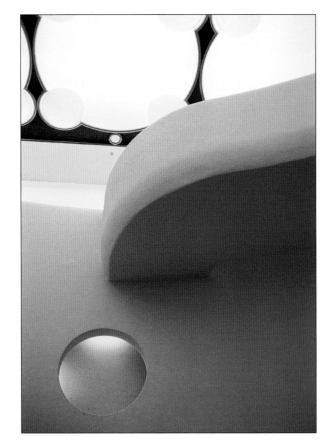

Right: Interior showing the ground floor, the ramp, and the top-lighting, which is diffused through the glass roof and enhanced by a series of hemispherical light forms and a further series of recessed circular lights.

Right: Interior view of the ramp, looking up into the top-lighting of the roof. The spiral form of the defining ramp, which extends through the two stories of the building, is echoed in the circular forms of the lighting and showcases.

134

Right: View of the exterior, across Maiden Lane. The site of the shop (now a gallery) is exceptionally narrow, and the dark, cave-like entrance gives little indication of the light-filled interior within, although lights can be glimpsed through the pattern of spaces in the fine brickwork.

Wright much admired. Wright emphasizes the treatment of the elegant brickwork of the façade with fine horizontal mortar joints. The spectator is drawn to the façade, which is entirely windowless when it is seen across the narrow street, and, on approaching, can admire the fine detail of the brickwork, which sets the shop apart from the surrounding buildings. Despite its age it has weathered particularly gracefully.

Once inside the shop, it is possible to see why the interior is often perceived as a forerunner of the Guggenheim Museum but on a smaller scale. The spiral form of the defining ramp of the interior, which extends through the two stories of the shop, is echoed in the circular forms that abound elsewhere in the interior design. The visitor ascends the ramp to view the objects set out in the elegant interior from changing vantage points, while further objects are displayed in a series of cases set into the concrete of the ramp. The subtle internal illumination of the display cases is enhanced by the extraordinarily sophisticated lighting of the entire interior. This is achieved by a characteristically Wrightian use of top-lighting diffused through the glass roof, which is further enhanced by a series of hemispherical light forms and a series of recessed circular lights, all of which contribute to the spacious ambience of the shop, belying its comparatively small space.

Above left: Solomon R. Guggenheim Museum, New York. View of the hemispherical dome from the ramp. The V.C. Morris Gift Shop is often seen as a small-scale forerunner of the Guggenheim Museum.

137

ORNAMENTATION AND DETAIL

Wright's extraordinary attention to

detail is manifest in every aspect of his work, even from the beginning of his career as an apprentice with Louis Sullivan. He believed that "a building should appear to grow easily from its site and be shaped to harmonize with its surroundings if Nature is manifest there, and if not, try to make it as quiet, substantial and organic as She would have ... were the opportunity Hers." This included both exterior and interior architectural detail, ranging from decorative urns and plaques, such as those that embellished his own Home and Studio in Oak Park, to the decoration of the hearth in homes as various as those designed in his early career and for the so-called "California Romanza," such as the Aline Barnsdall ("Hollyhock") House and the Ennis Brown House of the 1920s.

Above right: Samuel and Harriet Freeman House, Los Angeles, California. Detail of concrete block. The 16-inch square block is the unit of design for the building, whether perforated, solid, or filled with glass to form windows.

Right: Samuel and Harriet Freeman House. Hearth area of living room. Perforated and glazed blocks form a line of clerestory windows.

Right: Mabel and Charles Ennis House. The loggia of the grandest of Wright's California textile block houses uses square-within-a-square motifs, derived from Mayan temple architecture, throughout the dramatic interior.

Right: Mabel and Charles Ennis (Ennis Brown) House, Los Angeles, California. Glass mosaic overmantel in the colonnade. The wisteria motif and overall design is reminiscent of those produced by Orlando Giannini for Wright houses 30 years before.

The harmonization of the building with its surroundings is achieved on a new, suburban site such as Oak Park through the "quiet, substantial and organic" architectural form and decorative detail. On a site as dramatic as those for the Californian textile block houses, or indeed for such a dramatic site as that of the I.N. Hagan House (Kentuck Knob), different solutions were applied to make it "appear to grow easily from its site and be shaped to harmonize with its surroundings." Wright's lifelong adherence to his principle of an organic architecture had the consequence that no design element of his buildings, however small, remained unnoticed. This extended to the urns and vases he designed to literally contain nature within the houses, as well as the ceramics designed for specific buildings, such as the Imperial Hotel, Tokyo, and Midway Gardens.

The fact that ornamentation, like furnishings, was conceived of as part of the organic whole can be seen demonstrated in the design of the James Charnley House of Chicago, constructed in 1891. Wright's contribution can never be firmly established, but there are some elements of the imposing building that would suggest the hand of the fledgling architect. In later life, Wright was to claim to have been the principal designer of what he termed this "first modern building," although the preponderance of Sullivanesque elements in the design would seem to contradict this, and the truth will never be established with any clarity. However, it may well be that Sullivan gave Wright the major part of the design, and if this was so it is both significant and astonishing that an architect not yet 24 could create the grand exterior elevation that commands its city center site with such authority. Its dignity sets it apart from the buildings that surround it, which are built in the range of historical revival styles then fashionable. The ornamental detail of the exterior is remarkable for its elegance and refined use of materials, notably Roman brick, finely finished ashlar stone, and cast bronze, which give it an air of austere grandeur. In contrast, the carved interior decoration of the house is rich and complex. The grand oak staircases of the house are lit by a skylight using floriated motifs derived from Sullivan's design for the Auditorium Building.

Above: James Charnley House, Chicago, Illinois. Carved newel post of central stair. The carved decoration of the central staircase is in the style of Louis Sullivan, using motifs derived from leaf and plant forms.

Above left: James Charnley House, Chicago, Illinois. Detail of carved decoration of stair hall. The carved oak decoration of the grand central staircase is rich and complex in its figurative detailing.

Above: James Charnley House, Chicago, Illinois. Central stair hall. The stair hall has a distinctive baluster and staircage of thin, flat oak spindles in contrast to the rich floriate decoration.

Right: James Charnely House. Entrance façade and loggia. Constructed of Roman brick and finely finished ashlar stone, the austere grandeur of the façade is enriched with a second floor loggia, with classical columns and an elegant frieze.

Wright's first significant independent design, two years later in 1893, for the William H. Winslow House in River Forest, Illinois, represents a clear development in his career, indeed a watershed in his development. The front façade is built from dark brown terracotta with a Sullivanesque frieze that recalls plant forms at the upper levels, while gold-toned brick is used for the lower story. Its harmony, symmetry, and balance is in strictest contrast to the quirky rear elevation that has an octagonal stair tower, slender gothic-style widows, and angular lines of decorative brickwork. The interior of the house is no less remarkable, particularly in its use of wood. The hall arcade is a most distinctive feature with its prominent fireplace, inglenook, and subtle use of lighting. Wright's "sacred hearth" here achieves an extraordinary centrality to the whole house, raised as it is on a podium of three steps placed facing the entrance door, and designed on a scale that makes the inglenook and hearth a virtually independent space. The elegance of the slender columns and classical capitals that form the inglenook arcade,

Left: Harold C. Price Tower, Bartlesville, Oklahoma. Apartment interior showing the diamond motifs of the surface ornamentation, which extends to the copper-stamped cladding and chimney as well as the ceiling lights.

is enhanced by the carved decoration of the spandrels, and the frieze that has restrained floriated decoration containing heraldic motifs.

The notion of the "sacred hearth" was central to Wright's philosophy and forms a key aspect of his work, visible from the exterior in the form of a huge chimney, even in such an early commission as the Winslow House. Winslow House presents a synthesis of what might be termed Wright's early mature style in its simplification of forms, and its interior spaciousness and sense of repose. Wright believed that the design of houses should signify the private domain, the idea of shelter. This was in contrast to public buildings, which needed to symbolize power and success in terms of height. As he wrote, "the horizontal line is the line of domesticity…shelter should be the essential look of any dwelling." This radical idea was central to the Prairie house designs, first seen in the design for his own home and studio, and in the Winslow House, where the long, low lines of the house make it seem at one with its site. The huge chimney, which serves the "sacred hearth" and was central to Wright's ideal of family life can be read from the exterior, as it appears to offset the overwhelming horizontality of the design. Wright used exterior ornamental features to both offset and enhance the idea of shelter in his early houses, which included urns and sculptures, in both relief and free-standing forms, to mark the entrances.

The showcase studio addition he made to his own house in 1895 is a case in point. The studio complex forms a separate entity from the house. Although they are interconnected each has a separate entrance and a distinctive character of its own. Moving his practice from downtown Chicago to the affluent suburb, where most of his clients lived, was a decisive move, and one which Wright anticipated increasing his output by one third. The studio has a grand and complex entranceway for clients, quite separate from the family part of the house. Whereas the house itself is dominated by a massive, sheltering shingle-covered gable on the Forest Avenue façade, the studio complex, on Chicago Avenue, presents itself to the street as a series of vertical forms built of brick. A long, low loggia links the octagonal drafting room to the library, and the façade is embellished with sculptured plaques together with free-standing sculptures on top of the entrance piers. The stork

Left: William H. Winslow House, River Forest, Illinois. Hall arcade and inglenook. Three steps lead to the arcade, which houses the hearth and inglenook. The columns of the arcade are slender and classical in form, with carved capitals and elaborately carved spandrels.

Right: Frank Lloyd Wright Home and Studio, Oak Park, Illinois. Stork plaque at entrance to the studio. The four plaques were sculpted by Richard Bock from designs by Wright and show storks as symbols of fertility flanking a plan of the Roman Baths of Caracalla.

Right: Frank Lloyd Wright Home and Studio, Oak Park, Illinois. Living room fireplace and inglenook. For Wright the "sacred hearth" was the focal point of family life. Here the space could be curtained off. The paneled overmantel has cupboards flanking a carved homily.

Left: Frank Lloyd Wright Home and Studio. Playroom, looking toward the hearth and mural over the fireplace. The overmantel mural, by Orlando Giannini, represents the story of Aladdin and the genie of the lamp.

147

plaques and sculptures by Richard Bock, Wright's favored architectural sculptor, are an integrated part of the façade and serve to declare its artistic function. The geometric forms of the four urns that top the piers of the encircling wall are used throughout Wright's early domestic commissions.

The studio complex, and the adjoining house were completed by June 1898, establishing Wright's significant architectural presence in Oak Park. Until his flight from Oak Park in 1909, the site became the center of Wright's enterprise, and a powerhouse for his ideas. It is estimated that designs for some 162 buildings were produced from the modest complex and these were transmitted throughout the United States and Europe through publication.

A considerable photographic record exists of the original interior of the house, and the asymmetrical, organic arrangement of objects within it was subject to constant rearrangement. In 1904 Charles White wrote "the studio is again torn up by the annual repairs and alterations. Twice a year Mr. W. rearranges and changes the different rooms. He says he has gotten more education in experimenting on his own premises, than in any other way." Wright's compulsion to rearrange objects remained with him throughout his life. Nearly 60 years later Oligivanna Lloyd Wright wrote not only about the constant changing of the furniture at Taliesin East and Taliesin West but about short stays in hotels when they rearranged the furniture and "then we would go and buy flowers, branches or fruit to make the short stay as beautiful as it could

Above: Copper vase on the table of the library at the Frank Lloyd Wright Home and Studio, Oak Park, Illinois. The tall vases were designed to be filled with flowers, or even weeds, or dried flowers, as seen here.

Above: Frank Lloyd Wright Home and Studio. Detail of the drafting room fireplace. The design for the low-relief frieze panel seen here was used at the Heller House, Chicago, and represents the first collaborative work between Wright and the sculptor Richard Bock.

Left: Copper urn from the Dana House. Monumental urns were used to provide dramatic geometric emphasis, where needed, as part of an interior design.

be made in an impersonal hotel room." Among the first objects Wright designed were containers for branches and flowers, which are seen in a photograph of the Oak Park studio of 1898, together with the Japanese prints, ceramics, and other objects Wright collected throughout his life, which were placed in arrangements throughout the house for the benefit of family and students alike.

The designs for copper vases and urns, which were used as key components of the designs of the Oak Park years, were probably designed soon after 1893, at the start of Wright's independent practice. An article by Robert C. Spencer Jr., in the *Architectural Record* of June 1900, gives an account of a group of copper objects for which drawings exist: "Among the decorative things in the Oak Park Studio are some very interesting vessels and flower-holders of sheet copper of Mr Wright's design, always filled with masses of summer bloom or trophies of autumn fields and woods according to the season." Thus nature, essential to the concept of organic architecture, was brought inside.

The copper urn and weed holder designed at this period are among Wright's best-known early designs and are used throughout his interiors of the period. Wright's son, John Lloyd Wright, explained that his father was "not satisfied with the bric-a-brac of the day so he designed his own…The copper weed-holders …are his early creations. Father liked weeds!" The slender, angular form of the weed holder had a particularly long life, forming part of the Dana-Thomas House decoration, and appearing fifty years later in drawings by Wright for suggested interiors for Heritage-Henredon.

The large copper urn appears to have been first used in the Edward C. Waller House at River Forest, which Wright remodeled in 1899. A favored place for the urn was on the newel post of the staircase, where it appears in early photographs of the stair hall of the Waller House, its circular shapes complementing the pierced circular forms of the stair rail. It is used as a circular accent in the Dana-Thomas House, where the polished surface perfectly complements the autumnal palette used throughout the decoration of the house. Wright was to use the very particular qualities of copper throughout his life, both for artifacts and in the ornamentation of buildings: photographs and

Right: Marin County Civic Center, San Rafael, California. Details of the exterior and the interior light wells, showing the repeating circular and semicircular motifs that form the integrated design of the ornamentation and detail.

Left: Marin County Civic Center, San Rafael, California. Exterior view showing the organic and futuristic design of the form and ornamentation of this vast complex, which spans three hills.

Right: Sophie and Meyer May House, Grand Rapids, Michigan. Living room fireplace detail showing the mortar faced with thin bands of iridescent glass of harmonizing colors. In certain lights, the mortar appears to dissolve in the light and only the bricks remain.

surviving fragments of the demolished Imperial Hotel in Tokyo demonstrate that copper was used in combination with terracotta for both internal and external decoration of the vast building.

The urn, which was not cast, but made hammered into relief from the reverse side, was shown in 1902 at the Chicago Architectural Club where it was listed as a "repoussé bowl" made by the Chicago firm of James A. Miller and Brother, who worked on various Sullivan interiors. Over 20 years later in *In the Cause of Architecture* Wright was to give one of his rare insights into his working relationship with the craftsmen who produced his work, describing Miller as having "intelligent pride in his material and a sentiment concerning it…At that time I designed some sheet copper bowls, slender flower holders and such things, for him, and fell in love with sheet copper as a building material."

The design of the urn was geometric, using the flat forms of the Froebel Gifts as well as the more usual blocks in its overall circular shape, which rises from a cross base and uses a design of squares and inscribed circles on all four sides, which echo its shape. The urn was most often used to complement geometric designs and placed at eye level or above, where its forms can be most appreciated.

For his wealthy clients in River Forest and Springfield, in the Prairie house years, money was no object in the embellishment of the houses. The Dana-Thomas House has, for example, hand-stained decoration of sumac flowers worked directly into the sand-treated walls of the dining room. Sculpture was a prestigious embellishment of such interiors, in free-standing form or in the form of relief. At the Dana-Thomas House, Wright worked with the sculptor Richard Bock, who had pro-

vided the sculptural decoration for this own house and studio at Oak Park. In the "Flower in the Crannied Wall" and fountain sculptures, Bock was to provide some of his most memorable work.

Ten years later, Wright was to work with Richard Bock and the sculptor Alfonso Iannelli on the very different sculptural decorations for Midway Gardens. Wright himself provided the design for the female sprite at the entrance to the vast complex, while he worked in close collaboration with both sculptors on the other huge concrete figures, supervising their execution at each stage of their development. Richard Bock designed a large modeled relief for the Dining Room which was cast in concrete but, like so much of the sculpture at Midway Gardens, no longer exists. However, some of the sprites still survive, while heads of others may be found in private collections. Wright himself worked with Iannelli on the free-standing figures that can be seen in photographs of the main dining room. These giant figures held the geometric forms so precious to Wright: the sphere, cube, cone, and octagon. The geometric forms of the statues recall work by such European designers as Joseph Hoffmann, which Wright would have known from publication or perhaps have seen on his recent European travels. He explained their inspiration, "The lovely human figure might come into the scheme but come in only to respect the architecture."

Wright was given overall control of the complete design of Midway Gardens, although not all of the interior furnishings were made and very few survive the demolition of the Gardens in 1929, when most of the art works (which included murals, as well as sculpture), furnishings, and fittings were destroyed or sold. The most predictable loss perhaps

Above: Allen House, Wichita, Kansas. Detail of brickwork masonry joints. The horizontal masonry joints of the interior brickwork, or pointing of the house, is embellished with gold leaf to enhance the richness of the interior.

Above left: Frederick C. Robie House, Chicago, Illinois. Entrance façade. The horizontal planes of the design of the entire house are complemented by the geometric forms of the giant urn at the entrance.

Above: Details of two sculptures surviving from the Midway Gardens, Chicago. The large concrete sculptures of the entertainment complex were the joint effort of Wright and the sculptors Richard Bock and Alfonso Iannelli.

Right: Sculpture designed for the Midway Gardens, Chicago. One of several so-called "sprite" figures for the Summer Garden (which was destroyed along with the rest of the complex in 1929).

is that of the ceramics Wright designed for the several eating outlets in the gardens. From drawings, it would appear that Wright designed complete table settings of china, using square motifs, which are repeated in the table napkins and in the design of the square chairs, and even in the pattern of the floor covering. The design of the ceramics would seem to draw upon the confetti motifs from the Coonley Playhouse windows, with linked squares around the rim of the cup and saucer that survive in the collection of John Lloyd Wright, who wrote in his memoir of his father, "To me, all that marks the spot is a single white cup and saucer. Dotted around the rim of the saucer and mouth of the cup is a design of square confetti-like vermilion beauty spots. Dad designed it especially for the Gardens—I drew it—Shenango China made it."

The Imperial Hotel commission, which was begun in 1915, with the hotel opening in 1922, was another unrivalled opportunity for Wright to design an entirely integrated organic building, as the lavish and

Right: "Nakoma" glazed earthenware sculpture. Originally designed by Wright as one of a pair of monumental sculptures for an unrealized architectural project.

ambitious commission included all the furnishings together with ceramics and silver. The silver designs, of which rare examples survive, were for an angular shaped three-piece coffee service, hexagonal in form—a geometric device seen in the design throughout the hotel, even in the backs of the chairs and the occasional furniture.

The ceramics designed for the hotel had a happier fate and were in production until the 1960s, although production was interrupted during the Second World War. Wright's only previous design for ceramics had been for Midway Gardens, where he had used a pattern of squares, resembling confetti. For the Imperial Hotel services, Wright used a vibrant pattern of red, green, yellow, and blue overlapping disks that recalled in some measure the designs for the art-glass windows of the Coonley Playhouse, as well as making reference to specifically Japanese design motifs such as fans. Several versions of the design were made for use in the different dining spaces of the hotel, all containing an abstract "IH" Imperial Hotel monogram inscribed within one of the circles on each separate cup, bowl, or plate of the services. The earliest versions were made of fine porcelain, which was found to be inappropriate for the wear and tear of daily use in the prestigious hotel, and

the later services were made to withstand more robust wear.

In 1922, an elegant gold-rimmed pattern was designed for the formal dining room of the hotel, which is constructed from squares forming crosses, with a single pendant motif on the plates, bowls, and saucers that mirrors the geometric forms of the architecture and ornamentation of the entire building. Both designs have been reproduced for use today—a testament of their continuing appeal.

The circular motifs of Wright's ceramics, using red, his favorite color, appear also in the large, custom-made fireplace kettles for such clients as Edgar Kaufmann at Fallingwater and Herbert Johnson at "Wingspread." The centrality of the sacred hearth is a key element of all Wright's domestic designs, and in such elements as the fire kettles, grates, and andirons, at both Fallingwater and "Wingspread," Wright provided a further dramatic reinforcement red, the color of the earth, to the focal point of each building. The spherical kettles were designed to be hung from an arm with a complex system of hooks and supports over the open fire laid on the red iron grate. The kettles were designed to mull wine and cider and could be swung to one side of the fireplace when not in use.

Above: Dinner set, consisting of plate, bowl, cup, and saucer designed for the Imperial Hotel, Tokyo, c. 1922. Made by Noritake-Heinz & Co.

Above left: Plate designed for Midway Gardens, Chicago, 1913–14. Wright designed whole matching ceramic sets for the various eating places in the entertainment complex, all with matching geometric designs.

CASE STUDY: ISIDORE HELLER HOUSE

ISIDORE HELLER HOUSE, CHICAGO, ILLINOIS.
CONSTRUCTED 1896.

The Isidore Heller House was one of Wright's earliest commissions for a three-storied residence, and is of particular interest as a link in development between the so-called "finished attics" of his earliest work, and the fully evolved Prairie style. Together with the W. Irving Clark House of 1893, which has a third-floor ballroom on its front elevation, the Heller House anticipates a design seen later, at its most complex and complete, in the Frederick C. Robie residence of 1905. The disposition of its internal spaces might also be said to look forward to the design of the mature Prairie house, while the richness of its ornamentation and detail seem to anticipate the most lavish of the Prairie houses, the Susan Lawrence Dana (Dana-Thomas) House. The Heller House also demonstrates an early collaboration between Wright and the sculptor Richard Bock, a collaboration which was to continue until well after Wright left Illinois in 1909.

Right: Detail of third-story elevation. The sculptured capitals in Romanesque style are reminiscent of the floriated decoration seen in Louis Sullivan's buildings, including the Trading Room of the Chicago Stock Exchange and the Auditorium Building.

Right: Side elevation. The elaborate third-floor loggia is in distinct contrast to the plain, rather austere façade.

158

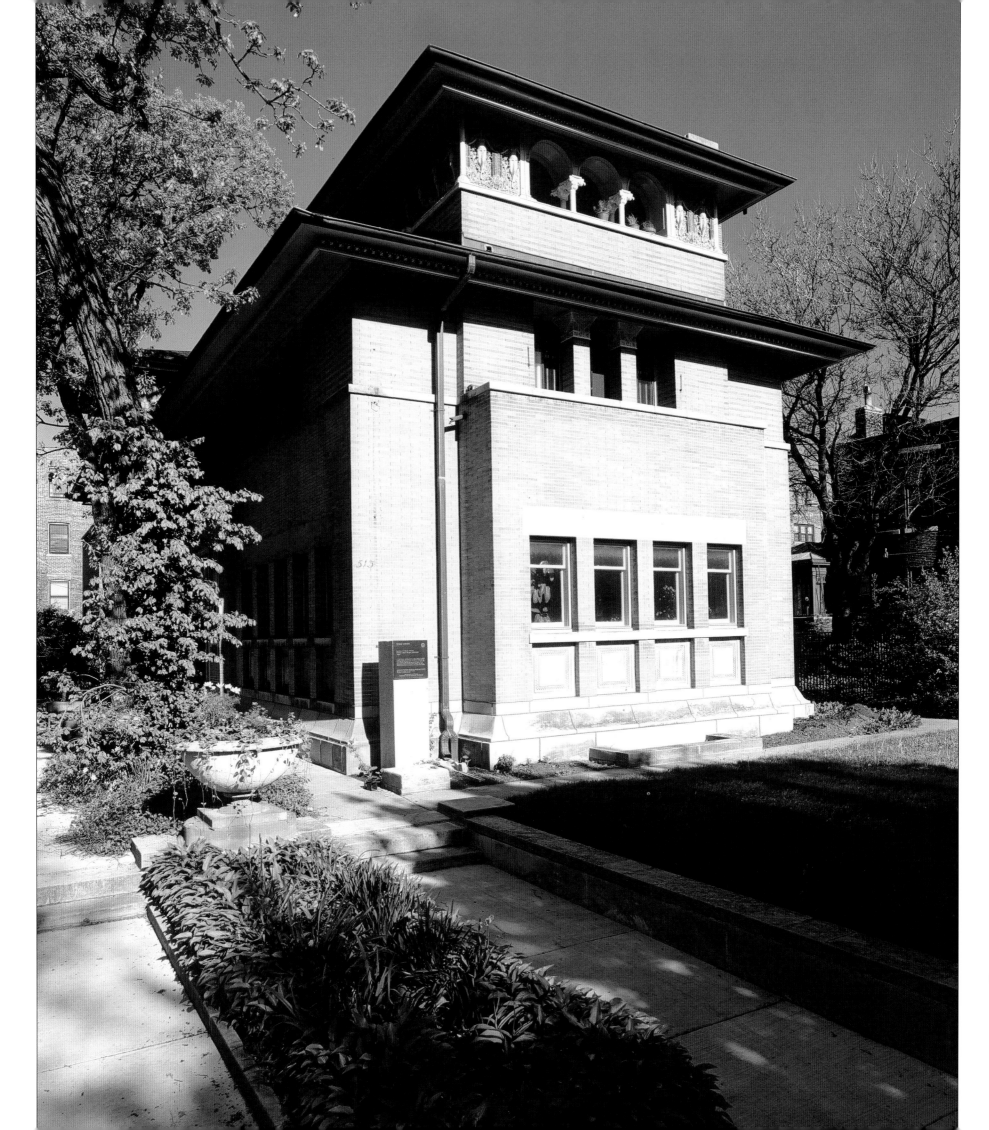

Right: The design for the low-relief frieze panel seen here (at Frank Lloyd Wright Home and Studio) was used at Heller House. It represents the first collaborative work between Wright and the sculptor Richard Bock.

The house is built on a restrictively cramped city site on the south side of Chicago, and is consequently long and narrow in plan with its elaborate entry not presented to the street, but on its southern side. It is among a small number of early Wright designs that are sometimes typified as a "monitor," meaning a third small story is added above the main projection of the eaves with its own hipped roof. Here the third story is elaborated by being partly enclosed to form a loggia with elaborate columns, which support the roof, and further decorated with sculptured reliefs by Richard Bock.

The inset porch, with its florid filigree decoration and ledges wide enough to support plant pots, is a curiously Sullivanesque extravaganza that is the greatest possible contrast to the comparative austerity of the rest of the façade, which is constructed of yellow Roman brick with white stone dressing. The interior materials consist in the main of waxed white oak and plaster in a rough sand finish that appears saturated with pure color, a decorative device used later in the Dana House. Other portions of the exterior elevation are embellished with a deep paneled frieze of a design, which might be termed Arabic in derivation, while the columns marking the entrance to the house are Romanesque in origin, the whole forming an extraordinarily eclectic design mix, unusual even in Wright's early work. It may be surmised that at this period, Wright was not able to exercise as much control on the wishes of some clients as he had been able to do with like-minded collaborators such as William Winslow, whose house he designed three years earlier. It may well be that the house as it stands could have represented a particular desire of the client for such an elaborate public statement.

The reliefs of the plaster panels by Richard Bock were adapted from Wright's designs for the book cover of a privately printed edition of "The Eve of St Agnes" by John Keats, which was bound by William Wilmslow in the same year the Heller House was built. The design was adapted to a different medium by Richard Bock, and Wright was so pleased with the result that one of the panels found its way into his studio, where it was put in a position of honor above the hearth.

Left: Decorative panels by the sculptor Richard Bock, following designs by Wright (which had originally been used as a book cover design) form a frieze along the loggia on the third story and are protected from adverse weather by the steep overhang of the eaves.

CASE STUDY: SUSAN LAWRENCE DANA (DANA-THOMAS) HOUSE

SUSAN LAWRENCE DANA (DANA-THOMAS) HOUSE.
SPRINGFIELD, ILLINOIS. CONSTRUCTED 1902.

The house built for the wealthy socialite Susan Lawrence Dana, for entertaining on a lavish scale and for housing a considerable art collection, was Wright's largest and most ornamental residence up until that time. Sculpture formed a key component of its embellishment from the original specification of the house. The most striking piece is the near-life-size terracotta sculpture by Richard W. Bock in the entrance hall. The enigmatic sculpture is formed from an abstracted female form, which most probably represents Wright's ideal of the Muse of Architecture. The figure appears to be tending a geometric form in the shape of a faceted, pylon-shaped structure, which rises from the same base and is an integral part of the same molded form. The sculpture presides over the entrance hall on a high plinth on which are inscribed the lines by Alfred, Lord Tennyson, which seem to have inspired the piece and which Wright had included in *The House*

Right: Dining room showing wall decoration. The frieze, like others in the house, uses decorative motifs drawn from the sumac, golden rod, and purple asters, and was painted into the sand-finished plaster by George Mann Niedecken.

Right: Fountain room and "Moon Children" sculpture by Richard Bock. The water in the wall fountain flows from an urn shaped like a full moon, which is encircled by "happy children's figures," in Bock's words.

Right: Entrance façade with urn. Wright used this monumental urn on its high plinth to lend further status to the curve of the entranceway. A similar urn is used on the garden front.

Beautiful, the influential book he had designed eight years before:

> Flower in the crannied wall,
> I pluck you out of the crannies,
> I hold you here, root and all, in my hand,
> Little flower—but if I could understand
> What you are, root and all, and all in all,
> I should know what God and man is.

Richard W. Bock wrote in his memoirs of the problems of realizing the sculpture, "Frank's idea for the figure was well conceived but far from solved…we frictionized and fraternized, often coming to the verge of tears in our arguments for Frank could not make up his mind how it should be done." When, as Bock relates, he finished the figure while Wright was away, Wright was delighted: "he beamed and threw his arms around me…you have done it, Dicky, you have done it. This is going to make you famous."

A complex terracotta relief forms a sculptural fountain in the fountain court, which is lit by some of the most splendid art glass in the house, in the form of a glass screen and flanking lighting fixtures. Bock called the fountain "the moon children," and it represented, in Bock's words, "a rising full moon with happy children's figures." The nude forms are inscribed within a circle and the source of the fountain flows from a circular urn. The conception and forms of the relief are much more conventional and of their time, whereas "Flower in the Crannied Wall," although bearing more than a vestige of classicism, is radical in comparison.

Wright was to develop the idea of standing forms in the huge Midway Gardens concrete-molded sculptures of nearly a decade later. Some of the "sprites" held the geometric forms so central to Wright's ethos of design and all were geometric in form, a joint effort of design between Wright and the sculptors Richard Bock and Alfonso Iannelli.

Left: Detail of exterior frieze. Wright's original designs for the exterior included a richly textured frieze cast in bronze. The lavish expenditure elsewhere in the house meant that the cheaper alternative of plaster, colored to emulate the patina of bronze, was used instead.

Right: "Flower in the Crannied Wall" sculpture, from the front. Richard Bock worked from Wright's designs for the finished terracotta after an earlier commission for the work had fallen through. The symbolic female figure nurtures a "skyscraper" building.

Right: "Flower in the Crannied Wall" sculpture seen from the back, beneath the butterfly transom at the entrance to the house. The sculpture, by Richard Bock, working to Wright's design, has the words of Tennyson's poem inscribed in a panel at the back.

167

CASE STUDY: ALINE BARNSDALL ("HOLLYHOCK") HOUSE

ALINE BARNSDALL ("HOLLYHOCK") HOUSE, LOS ANGELES, CALIFORNIA. DESIGNED 1918, CONSTRUCTED 1920–21.

Hollyhock House was one of Wright's most ambitious projects, and the difficulties of realizing its design were exacerbated by the fact that Wright was working on the Imperial Hotel, Tokyo, during the project and his client, an oil heiress who managed a theater, was traveling too. As Wright later explained, "Hollyhock House had mostly to be built by telegraph so far as client and architect had anything to do with it or each other." Wright wrote in his autobiography of the genesis of the extraordinary style and design of the house. In several senses Hollyhock House may be said to have been the first of Wright's Californian houses to establish a new typology in his work, one that was particularly responsive to regional and cultural circumstances that were so very different to the Prairie houses. A major factor in Wright's attraction to the region was his sense that it was a desert that could

Right:. Detail of the roofline of the exterior, showing the dominant hollyhock motifs used as turrets and towers to form a futuristic and fantastical skyline.

Right: Main façade. The form and motifs of the Barnsdall residence are reminiscent of Mayan temple structures, freely interpreted as a realization of a dream or fantasy, drawing on the particular spirit of the place as well as the client's wishes.

be changed out of recognition, and that both symbolically and historically related to pre-Columbian culture. Thus the motifs of the Barnsdall
residence are reminiscent of Mayan temple structures, albeit freely
interpreted in Wright's inimitable manner.

Writing some years after the house was built, in *An Autobiography*,
Wright recalled the extraordinary opportunities the commission
presented:

> "So, when called upon by Aline Barnsdall—her métier the theater—to
> build a house for her in Hollywood, why not make architecture stand
> up and show itself on her new ground, known as Olive Hill, as
> Romance? A bit sentimental, Miss Barnsdall had pre-named the house
> for the Hollyhock she loved for many reasons, all of them good ones,
> and called upon me to render her favorite flower as a feature of
> Architecture how I might."

The use of the stylized hollyhock motif was carried out in an extraordinarily thorough-going manner, in both the ornamentation of the
structure itself and the style and design of such integrated elements as
the dining room chairs and tables. It also appears in the coloration of
the art-glass windows, using a palette, unique in Wright's work, of purple, mauve, and green. Most extraordinary of all, perhaps, is the central
feature of the living room, the "sacred hearth" lit by a dramatic skylight
above, a wooden light screen with hollyhock motifs to direct the
Californian sunlight in to the room in a suitably theatrical manner. The
symmetrical forms of the skylight are reflected in a shallow pool, and
both skylight and pool are rectilinear in form, echoing the prevailing
hollyhock motifs throughout the house. In contrast, the relief mural of
the fireplace uses overlapping circles and squares, reminiscent of the
forms Wright was using in the Imperial Hotel commission. The relief
mural of the overmantel, though abstract in form, is purported to be a
representation of Aline Barnsdall as a princess of Amerindian myth, in
one of Wright's most extraordinary flights of fantasy.

Right: Exterior detail showing the
stylized hollyhock motifs that are the
dominant motif of the house. The
opalescent and art glass of the windows carries through the hollyhock
design in the form of petals.

Left: Living room hearth and skylight. The skylight crowns the central hearth of the house, which is reflected in a shallow pool. The distinctive overmantel bears a carved abstraction, purportedly of Aline Barnsdall as a princess of Amerinidian myth.

CASE STUDY: HERBERT F. JOHNSON HOUSE ("WINGSPREAD")

HERBERT F. JOHNSON HOUSE ("WINGSPREAD") WIND
POINT, WISCONSIN. CONSTRUCTED 1937.

"Wingspread" built for Hebert F. "Hib" Johnson, grandson of the founder of Johnson's Wax, and its president, was Wright's largest and most expensive domestic commission to date. The center of the pinwheel layout of the house is the monumental brick chimney stack that is the core of the building and a reworking of the principle of Wright's "sacred hearth" on a grand scale. It has no less than five fireplaces that divide the vertical space into areas, in Wright's words, "for the various domestic functions: Entrance Hall, Family Living Room, Library Living Room and Dining Room."

The stability and centrality of the living area is reflected in the detail as well as the design elements of the space, which reflect the shape of the room itself, juxtaposing hexagonal and circular motifs. The building materials themselves—finely detailed brickwork, large expanses of oak veneer, together with beautifully crafted sandstone detail and exceptionally finely crafted furniture—provide the essential ornamentation of the house; a key example of Wright's attention to detail and of skillfully worked, organic materials being used in an honest and natural state.

This can be readily perceived in both the built-in and free-standing furniture, which is of especially fine craftsmanship. The handsome barrel chairs, which had first been designed for the Darwin C. Martin House of 1904, are a case in point. Wright adapted the design specifically for Wingspread and juxtaposed its curves with the curve of the central chimney stack, the staircase, and other circular elements of the wholly integrated design. The curved forms are set against angled shapes: that of the central octagon of the building is echoed in the hexagonal hassocks and other similarly angled elements of the design, while the square grid, on which the house is built, is incised into the waxed concrete floors. Similar square forms run throughout the fenestration of the space: light falls from above, from a series of clerestory windows, while at different levels French windows open on to the terraces. The entire house is so oriented that sunlight falls in all of the spaces of the house.

It is recorded that the design process for the built-in components and the free-standing furniture was a particularly detailed one, with Wright's original drawings being submitted to Herbert Johnson at Taliesin before the detailed drawings were "expanded" by apprentices and submitted to the Gillen Woodwork Corporation of Milwaukee, Wisconsin, who also manufactured the fine furniture for Fallingwater.

The curvilinear forms of the brick chimney and the dramatic curved stair behind it, that leads to the observation tower, are further reinforced by the large metal kettle on the hearth. The kettle, with its specially designed apparatus, was also used to embellish the central hearth at Fallingwater, where it is colored Cherokee red. At Wingspread the kettle and fittings are black, in keeping with the sober detail of the rest of the space.

Right: Fireplace kettle. The first of a series of specially designed kettles and fireplace accoutrements.

172

INDEX AND PICTURE CREDITS

ACKNOWLEDGMENTS

All photography was taken by Simon Clay (© Chrysalis Images), including the cover photography, with the exception of the photographs on the following pages:

Page 6 (left) courtesy of The Metropolitan Museum of Art, Edward Pearce Casey Fund, 1982. (1982.1051.1);

Page 8 courtesy of © Ezra Stoller/ESTO/Arcaid;

Page 9 courtesy of © The Frank Lloyd Wright Foundation;

Page 18 courtesy of The Froebel Archive for Childhood Studies, University of Surrey, England;

Page 21 courtesy of © Carol M Highsmith;

Page 30 (bottom) courtesy of © Matt Phalen;

Page 60 (bottom) courtesy of the SC Johnson Company;

Page 62 (left), 64, 65, 149, 156 and 157 (left and right), courtesy of © V&A Picture Library;

Pages 66 (photograph courtesy of Thomas A. Heinz) and 67 courtesy of Western Pennsylvania Conservancy;

Page 76 courtesy of The Metropolitan Museum of Art, Purchase, Edgar J Kaufmann Foundation and Edward C Moore, Jr. Gifts, 1967 (67.231.1-.3). Photograph © 1978 The Metropolitan Museum of Art;

Page 83 courtesy of © Alan Weintraub/Arcaid;

Pages 112 (left and right), and 152 courtesy of Steelcase, Inc.;

Page 144 courtesy of Paul Rocheleau.